ALSO BY PAUL BENNETT, PhD, CFP®

Financial Economics of Index Annuities
An Analysis of Investor Returns

Easy Essays on Economics
Concise Coverage of Complex Concepts

Advance Praise for *The Money Navigator*

"This book is vitally important for anyone seeking financial confidence. I've spent thirty years in the investment business working with a variety of advisors, small and large. This is the first book I've read that is accessible to everyone. The information is so necessary, especially in these challenging financial markets. Read this book—over and over. You will be happy you did when it comes to making those important financial decisions in your life."

—Beverly D. Flaxington
The Human Behavior Coach® and bestselling author

"The financial landscape is strewn with obstacles that complicate making good decisions and achieving financial success. Most people need a helping hand to guide them on this journey. Paul Bennett's *The Money Navigator* provides that guidance by bringing more self-awareness to your financial life. If you are interested in receiving a high return on your investment, reading this book is an excellent way to attain that objective."

—H. Kent Baker, PhD, CFA, CMA
University Professor of Finance, American University;
Coauthor of *Investment Traps Exposed: Navigating Investor Mistakes and Behavioral Biases*

"In *The Money Navigator*, Paul Bennett introduces readers to a life-changing paradigm of financial life management called 'FinLife.' Based on cutting-edge research in the psychological sciences and Paul's own expertise as a financial advisor, this wonderful book will challenge readers to think differently about their financial lives and better about their entire lives."

—Barnaby B. Riedel, PhD
Co-Founder of Riedel Strategy

"The Money Navigator, Paul Bennett's third book, is his magnum opus. His most personal work to date, this book offers advice on topics as diverse as selecting an adviser, navigating the murky waters of investment products, and making sound financial decisions. The perfect book for the student of both markets and personal betterment."

—Daniel Crosby, Ph.D.
New York Times bestselling author of *The Laws of Wealth: Psychology and the Secret to Investing Success*

"Paul Bennett provides a wonderful new perspective into understanding money psychology and improving your financial outcomes. I found this book to be a highly instructive, enjoyable, and noteworthy 'how-to-guide' of behavioral finance."

—Victor Ricciardi
Co-editor of *Investor Behavior: The Psychology of Financial Planning and Investing*

The Money Navigator

The Money Navigator:

The Essential Guide to Living Your Ideal Financial Life

Paul C. Bennett, PhD, CFP®

GREENLEAF
BOOK GROUP PRESS

Published by Greenleaf Book Group Press
Austin, Texas
www.gbgpress.com

Distributed by Greenleaf Book Group

For ordering information or special discounts for bulk purchases, please contact Greenleaf Book Group at PO Box 91869, Austin, TX 78709, 512.891.6100.

Design and composition by Mark T. Farmer
Cover design by Mark T. Farmer

Cataloging-in-Publication data is available.

Print ISBN: 978-1-62634-441-9

eBook ISBN: 978-1-62634-442-6

Part of the Tree Neutral® program, which offsets the number of trees consumed in the production and printing of this book by taking proactive steps, such as planting trees in direct proportion to the number of trees used: www.treeneutral.com

TreeNeutral

Printed in the United States of America on acid-free paper

17 18 19 20 21 22   10 9 8 7 6 5 4 3 2 1

First Edition

To my Life Navigators:
Trissi, Chloe, and Luke

Acknowledgments

Anyone who has authored a book knows that the process can be a lonely and arduous experience at times. I liken it to running a marathon: You have periods of great success and other periods where you feel as though you may never finish. Fortunately I had an amazing support structure in place, so the writing process felt less isolated and was actually incredibly collaborative.

My amazing coach, Beverly Flaxington, was instrumental in keeping me focused on the end goal of completing the book while adhering to the core values of the Money Navigator. Bev has a true gift, which she tactfully and consistently utilized to challenge my ideas and ultimately squeeze more creativity out of me than I ever thought possible.

Without question, Joe Duran has inspired me to think bigger. What he has accomplished in the financial services industry is exceptional and continues to impress his peers, competitors, and colleagues alike. Joe is always on the cutting edge—heck, he often establishes the cutting edge—of where the industry is headed next. I feel extremely fortunate to call Joe my friend and business partner.

Leslie Dunham is so quick with her wit and flush with creative ideas. I would have been lost if not for Leslie's amazing ideas for spreading the word about The Money Navigator.

The Team at the Great Falls, Virginia office of United Capital has shown me for over ten years how impactful a group of Money Navigators can be on the lives of clients, with whom they work on a daily basis. Passionate professionalism reigns supreme with this team!

The team at Greenleaf Book Group has provided unwavering clarity end-to-end, from editing all the way through to publishing *The Money Navigator*. I am forever grateful for your knowledge and expertise.

Finally, Jimmy Moock and the team at Gregory FCA have been critical to establishing credibility and maintaining awareness of *The Money Navigator's* central message. You guys are real pros!

"Your net worth to the world is usually determined by what remains after your bad habits are subtracted from your good ones."
—Benjamin Franklin

Table of Contents

Foreword

Albert Camus famously said, "Life is the sum of all your choices." Unfortunately very few of us are taught how to make smart decisions, especially when it comes to money. As a consequence, we sometimes end up making choices we regret. Paul Bennett has written a book that will change that. It is a smart, clear perspective on how to optimize your decisions.

Paul has spent his entire career helping people look beyond their investments and focusing on decisions they can control. Whereas typical advisors focus on the market and investments, Paul has always focused on the person and helping them to improve their entire lives. In this book he shares clear steps to help ensure you can live your One Best Financial Life® right now.

I have known Paul for many years and have always been personally and professionally inspired by his calm, practical, and empathetic perspective. His genuine concern for the well-being of the people he comes into contact with is palpable, and I am thrilled he has written a book that discusses helping even more people improve their lives.

In *The Money Navigator*, you will learn about your inherent biases around money. The book will help guide you toward better decisions and greater financial well-being. Most importantly, Paul also provides helpful and concrete examples of how to put this new approach into action!

—Joe Duran CFA
CEO and Founder, United Capital
Newport Beach, CA 2017

Preface

This is the third book I have written, and it was by far the most personally gratifying. The reason I enjoyed it so much was due to the free-flowing nature of the process. The difference between *The Money Navigator* and *Financial Economics of Index Annuities* or *Easy Essays on Economics*, my two previous books, is the latter two were technical reads and this one is a true work of passion written for the purpose of helping you live your ideal financial life (FinLife®).

I can't begin to tell you how fun it was getting up at 0-dark-thirty, grabbing a cup of joe, and firing up the laptop to start putting my thoughts down on paper. What I mean by free-flowing is I literally wrote portions of the book based on what inspired me that day and then patched it all together like a quilt over the course of a year or so to create the finished mosaic. Sure, some parts I wrote never made it into the book, but that is the beauty of the creative process—kind of like painting versus sculpting—sometimes it's additive and sometimes it's subtractive!

My goal for the book is that anyone who picks up a copy and reads it can decide what it means to them and, as a result, have it make a positive impact in their FinLife®. I really hope you are motivated by and enjoy the end result, which I've called ***The Money Navigator***!

Introduction

*"We have another chance to navigate, perhaps in a slightly different way
than we did yesterday. We cannot go back. But we can learn."*
—*Jeffrey R. Anders,*
THE NATURE OF THINGS—NAVIGATING EVERYDAY LIFE WITH GRACE

"Have you plugged it into the navigation system?" or "Did you check Google Maps or Waze?" You hear this all the time these days. You are pressed for time, trying to get from point A to point B, and you want to make sure your trip is successful so you don't waste precious minutes by taking an unnecessary turn or encounter an avoidable delay by running into bad traffic. Navigating your financial life ("FinLife®") is a similar process. Unfortunately, unlike Google Maps and the like, there is no reliable GPS for making the right financial decisions.

We are currently in the midst of massive social and cultural changes and shifts. Thanks to the Internet, information has become amazingly accessible and enormous in size and scope. The playing field has been leveled so that access to information is no longer something for which a premium can be charged. In fact, information has become so easy to obtain that it has become commoditized and devalued. As a society we can get caught up in a quest for more and more information. Unfortunately, more often than not, this quest results not in more knowledge obtained, but in decision paralysis: As it turns out, *having too many choices causes real problems!* Information does not equal education. Having access is not enough—you must know how to apply what you have learned. Humans desire to have information that is contextualized to our particular wants and needs. Although technology has provided us with time, that ever-precious commodity, we have filled this freed-up time with even *more* work, making the ability to sift through and make sense of the endless expanse of information at our fingertips all the more difficult.

Consequently, while access to information has increased, knowledge about what to do and how to make the best decisions has not increased commensurately. If you think about the information you have related to your finances, you may wonder how exactly to make sense of it all. How do you deal with all of the financial choices out there? Will you be able to retire on your terms and time frames? How does technology play into your FinLife® and overall financial well-being? How can you become more engaged so you are confident about your financial future? "There has to be a better way," you might say to yourself. The good news: There *is* a better way. Fortunately, in reading this book, you've come to the right place to find the answers you need.

I wrote this book to help people understand the importance of working with a credentialed financial advisor, and more specifically, a CFP® professional who I call the **Money Navigator**. A Money Navigator can help you improve your decision making regarding anything having to do with your FinLife®. As you'll soon read, FinLife® decisions are not purely financial decisions. Most life choices have some financial impact—deciding what job to take, where to live, how long to work, and the like seem nonfinancial in nature, but they have financial ramifications. As just one example, most people divorce because of the relationship, but the impact is often felt in the pocketbook. There is no decision that is not connected, somehow, to your financial well-being. An experienced CFP® professional, a Money Navigator, can help you improve your decision making so you can live your Ideal FinLife®.

For the most part, I maintain a sense of informality throughout the book. There are some technical sections and advanced subject matter that require more in-depth thought, but overall I'd like you to feel as if you are having an authentic conversation with someone you trust. My goal is to make you feel as though we are talking on a Saturday afternoon at a neighborhood barbeque, chatting on the sidelines at your kid's soccer game, or discussing life in between holes of golf. I hope you find you are relaxed and open to hearing some new ideas that can impact your personal FinLife®.

How This Book Is Organized

It is my hope that after reading this book, you'll walk away with a better understanding of human behavior, the many reasons why investors make poor decisions, why financial and insurance products are so misunderstood, and why the average person needs a Money Navigator, a full-scale CFP® professional, to invest well and manage their FinLife®. Throughout the book I use real-life examples of situations I have encountered as a financial advisor over the past twenty-five-plus years. I also incorporate research I have personally conducted on the subject of common investor decision traps, but I do so in such a way that you can see how the research may apply to you personally.

Although the principles outlined in this book can be utilized by just about anyone, the book was primarily written for investors who are on the cusp of retiring, already in retirement, or facing a life transition, such as a career or job change, disability, financial windfall, divorce, or death of a loved one. Each chapter of the book provides you with practical takeaways for your particular situation, and regardless of which of the three categories of readers you fall into, as you read the book, my goal is for you to feel as though the book was written specifically for you and your unique set of circumstances.

The book is organized into four straightforward sections, as follows:

Section I, The Age of the Money Navigator, introduces you to the book's key ideas—Your FinLife®, the Money Navigator, and behavioral finance. Chapter 1 dives into the many factors that define and orient your FinLife® over time, clarifies the core characteristics of the Money Navigator, and demonstrates how those characteristics can help serve you and your financial future. Chapter 2 describes the differences between traditional and behavioral finance and how the latter relates to your FinLife®, setting you up for further exploration in the next section.

Section II, Navigating Your Decision Traps, provides a comprehensive overview of the many factors that determine—and undermine—your financial decision making. Chapter 3 explains how you can become more self-aware of the ways in which those factors outside of your control, such as which generation we were born into or our birth order, influence your FinLife®, while chapter 4 outlines how self-awareness of those factors within our control can lead to better financial decision making. Chapter

5 takes stock of the ways in which information overload can inhibit smart choices and describes how both you and your Money Navigator can overcome this barrier by thinking creatively toward solutions.

Section III, The Financial Services Industry Landscape, takes the idea of information overload further by introducing you to the many products and services that promise to push your FinLife® in the right direction—and shows you how a Money Navigator can help you choose wisely. Chapter 6 outlines the types of investment choices you could and should be making. Chapter 7 continues the dialogue by outlining the tools and methods available to you and weighing the pros and cons of each. Chapter 8 addresses the elephant in the room: What exactly is the difference between a Money Navigator and a regular financial planner, and why should you care? It turns out, you should care about these differences quite a bit—your financial future relies upon it!

Section IV, The Money Navigator in Depth, ties it all together: After learning more about the many pitfalls that can lead to a less-than-ideal FinLife® come retirement, from decision traps to information overload to subpar products on the market, the choice to find a Money Navigator becomes too clear to ignore. Chapter 9 outlines what you can expect from your relationship with your Money Navigator and gives you more reasons to find one now. Chapter 10 solidifies the value add of the Money Navigator, leaving no doubt in your mind that with a navigator by your side, your FinLife® has nowhere to go but up.

With the right navigation, arriving at your desired destination becomes not only possible, but highly likely! You have come to the right place in reading *The Money Navigator*, as the insights gleaned from the pages that follow cannot help but successfully propel you on your journey toward your Ideal FinLife®; remember, the journey is the best part of reaching your final destination!

The Age of the Money Navigator

"True navigation begins in the human heart.
It's the most important map of all."

—*Elizabeth Kapu'uwailani Lindsey*

CHAPTER 1

The Money Navigator and Your FinLife®

"If your actions inspire others to dream more, learn more,
do more, and become more, you are a leader."
—Dolly Parton

The aim of this book is to bring more self-awareness to your financial life (FinLife®) and to show you the ways in which a CERTIFIED FINANCIAL PLANNER™ can help you achieve your goals. As you know from the preface, I like to call the CFP® professional your own personal Money Navigator. But before we can dive into the ways in which a Money Navigator can assist you in your FinLife®, we must first define the terms. What *is* a Money Navigator exactly? What *is* your FinLife®? This chapter answers those basic questions and sets you up to learn more about your own human behavior and decision making. Let's begin!

The Money Navigator usually has a specialty focus. For example, the Money Navigator may focus his practice on individuals who are nearing retirement or already retired. As you get closer and closer to retirement, you are going through a transition, similar to climbing up a mountain and then coming back down. The Money Navigator is a master storyteller. Storytelling has a way of making things resonate for most so that you can put yourself in the shoes of the individuals who are part of the narrative. Indulge me for a couple of minutes so you can see how this makes sense and helps the points the Money Navigator makes resonate.

Sir Edmund Hillary was the first person to climb Mount Everest and more specifically to reach the summit. He accomplished this amazing feat in the early '50s with the help of his Nepalese Sherpa, mountaineer Tenzing Norgay. Most people have never heard of George Mallory, who almost thirty years earlier took part in an expedition to climb Mount Everest. Mallory never made it back down the mountain that day, but the question remains as to whether or not he reached the summit. His body was found in 1999 during an expedition that was specifically organized to find Mallory's remains. Mallory's remains were found below the summit. However, he had rappelling gear on, which indicated that he was on his way *down* the mountain. Interestingly, he had previously told his daughter that if he should reach the summit he would leave a photograph of his wife there. When his body was discovered, all of his clothing was intact, as were documents in his wallet. However, the photograph was missing. This fact opens the possibility that he did, in fact, reach the summit. The problem was that Mallory didn't make it down the *descent*, which any mountaineer will tell you is the most critical part of the climb. In fact, most mountain climbing deaths occur during the descent phase. What ended up setting Sir Edmund Hillary apart from Mallory? It's not so much *what*, but *whom*: Tenzing Norgay, Hillary's Sherpa!

My point of telling you this story is your FinLife® prior to retirement is like climbing a mountain, but that is only half of the battle. You need to successfully make it down the descent. Liken the descent to the distribution phase when you need retirement income during your FinLife® journey. The descent is far too important to not have a Money Navigator serving as your personal Sherpa!

Going to see your CFP® professional should be fun, enlightening, and engaging. Unfortunately, for most individuals, it is more like going to the dentist to have a procedure performed. When you visit your financial advisor, does she whip out a legal pad and start taking notes as you confess your financial sins? Are you ready to take a nap as he tells you the latest advances in modern portfolio theory or interest rate trends? This type of approach no longer works in today's conceptual society.

In today's culture, the financial advisor who provides a bespoke experience that is engaging, experiential, and personal will rise to the top of the profession. It must be appealing to you to work with your financial advisor, and it should also be fun and interactive. Your experience should be one where you are not being preached to; rather it should be participative, as you should be able to dynamically "pull the levers and turn the dials" that drive your financial plan. If your advisor prints out a financial plan the size of a New York City phone book, run the other way, fast! The problem with this is that the second the ink hits the page, the plan is outdated. Instead, what-if scenario testing should come into play here, and this is all done interactively on your financial advisor's flat screen or via an app on your phone! Gamification should also be included, which involves interactive exercises that help you get to the core of your money mind or philosophy about money, if you will.

The Money Navigator who brings a bionic experience to you (the melding of a robo-advisor, which is a DIY, or do-it-yourself method of financial planning via web-based tools and interfaces, married with a human being—see chapter 6 for more detail) is on the cutting edge of technology but not to the detriment of you losing the necessary human touch that machines simply cannot ever replicate.

The Money Navigator should be equipped with the right professional tools (see chapter 7) but should also bring humility, curiosity, and a human element into the equation in a way that helps you to understand why you feel the way you do about money. He helps you recognize that in life there are trade-offs and, as a result, ramifications. He can articulate specifically what the trade-offs mean to you and your ability to achieve your goals and objectives in the short and long term. The Money Navigator who is humble and curious and brings truth, discipline, and understanding to your experience is this advisor.

Thinking about Your FinLife®: Yesterday vs. Today

Before we dive any further into the Money Navigator himself, let's first outline his primary focus: your FinLife®. To understand how FinLife® works, my company hired a team of researchers to talk to our clients about money and what really matters to them. The findings were eye-opening and they made me better understand what it is you may be concerned about or striving for with respect to your FinLife®.[1]

As a result of the research, I realized that your FinLife® isn't just about money—rather it encompasses your entire life experience. The researchers

---

1   Reidel, B. (2015). Internal survey instrument conducted by Reidel Strategy. Newport Beach, CA.

had our clients talk about the chapters of their financial lives. If you had been part of the research, perhaps chapter one in your FinLife® book may have been your first job mowing lawns, for example. Your second chapter may have entailed working as a waitress during college to help pay for tuition, and your third chapter was your first job out of college working for an accounting firm. Included in the chapters would be the things that money enabled you to do during those times. Maybe you bought albums and chewing gum with your lawn mowing money, paid for tuition and a beer here and there with your waitress money, and paid rent and bought a new car with your accounting salary. The takeaway from this part of the research was that *working* and *spending* were far more important to most people than saving and investing. The irony of this is that the financial industry bombards you with advertising and marketing all about *saving* and *investing*; no wonder this makes you turn a deaf ear. As our research confirmed, you are more concerned about your ability to work and spend than your ability to save and invest.

Another takeaway from the study is that *your FinLife® is a series of trade-offs*. You realize that if you want something for your family, like private school for the kids for example, something else has to give. Perhaps that "something else" is choosing to move into a smaller house so that private school is an option and you can still retire on time and on your terms. The stories of over 80% of those surveyed in the study involved trade-offs in one way, shape, or form.

The final piece of insight I gleaned from the study of our clients' financial lives is that your financial decisions need *to be in line with your ideal self*. If not, a disconnect automatically occurs, which causes internal conflict, which results in you moving away from financial happiness. We will discuss why happiness is so important later in the book. If your financial decisions are in sync with your personal values, then you are happier than when you simply have more money. Money is not the "end all," but ***money-value alignment is truly ideal***.

How your innate human biases impact your decision making is of paramount importance. Further in the book, I will review the many decision traps you may face and how to avoid or minimize their impact. I'll also review how you make sure that, given your biases, your money serves your life's goals. This helps you answer the question of "what is it that you want your money to do for you?"

The type of financial support people require has changed with the times. If we take a closer look at yesterday's thinking, we see the information age, where left-brain thinking paid a significant amount of attention to text, or books that were studied. Again, information was critical—"what does this mean?" In today's conceptual age, we look more toward context, which provides us with the answer to "what does this mean to *me*?" Yesterday, we craved functional, whereas in today's right-brain, conceptual-driven culture, we look more toward the aesthetic, as functionality is a given. For instance, think of how Steve Jobs demanded that the first iPhone not only function superbly, but also *look* amazing as well. Logical thought is yesterday-driven, whereas empathetic thought is valued in today's society. It's not only about the numbers! Compassion or "empathy in action" is desired today. Step by step, sequential thinking dominated yesterday's culture, and now we crave simultaneous interaction and collaboration. What this means is that when facing decisions in the past, we often utilized a chronological progression in a silo-like fashion, whereas today we hunger for our information silos to interact and talk to each other. An example of this in practice is how the Money Navigator quarterbacks your Ideal FinLife®—he interacts and exchanges information with your other advisors, such as your CPA, attorney, and insurance agent. This collaboration results in better outcomes for you, as everyone can get on the same page. Similarly, a linear structure was valued in the past, but now a view of the big picture or macro is in demand. Finally, and in my opinion most importantly, professional was yesterday's requirement, but today's culture is yearning for authenticity. No more starch-shirted advice; it's time to bring on the backyard barbeque advisor. Someone who can tell you like it is while you are flipping burgers, drinking a beer, and watching the kids play. That someone has a gentle, authentic swagger. That someone is the *Money Navigator*!

Leadership Styles: Yesterday vs. Today

Individuals of every era have needs that differ greatly from years past in terms of what is necessary for success. To address these needs, different leadership styles emerge and evolve according to societal attitudes and the general economics of the time. The most successful leaders of any era are the ones that adapt quickly and coherently to the needs of the time. The Money Navigator is one such leader of our contemporary age. I am going to briefly summarize the evolution of leadership styles to provide some context in order to gain a better understanding of why the leadership style of Money Navigator is needed today.

Over the past couple of centuries, our culture in the United States has evolved from an agrarian-based economy to an industrial economy and then to a service economy. We are now on the tail end of the information age and rapidly growing into the conceptual age. In order to better understand why and how the leadership style exemplified by the Money Navigator emerged, let's briefly review where we have been as a nation with respect to the attitude of society, the economics of the time, and subsequently the type of leadership that was desired. This exercise will help you realize the type of leadership that is desired today, which I posit is the Money Navigator.

The 1950s were clearly a time of industrial advancement and economic expansion. Most people believe this tremendous growth stage, which spanned several decades, was due to the post–World War II economic boom. Why wouldn't this be the case? After all, the United States had significantly increased its industrial capacity due to the assembly lines, manufacturing processes, and production facilities we had built to feed the war machine. Additionally, financing became more popular and accessible, which enabled families to have new appliances in their homes and buy automobiles, resulting in the middle class becoming a force to be reckoned with economically.

Now do you want to know what actually acted as the catalyst for the growth boom in the '50s and '60s? The United States had just won the war. This means someone *lost* the war. That someone was Japan and Germany, the other two top economic superpowers in the world at that time. In winning World War II, the United States had literally just decimated the physical infrastructure and thereby the economies of these two powerful nations. We were the only game in town, so to speak, and as a result we flourished and our economy grew. As this phenomenon occurred, a certain type of leadership evolved, which was considered a command and control style. This was a direct result of the military style of leadership used in fighting the war. Whoever was at the top was the authority and figurehead of what to do and not to do. This leadership style had staying power and overlapped into the '60s and '70s.

In the 1970s, we saw an attitudinal shift toward self-help and self-motivation. Narcissistic behavior wove its way through the cultural phenomena of the time, such as the self-indulgent disco music scene—think

Saturday Night Fever. It was the "I'm okay, you're okay" time, but economically the '70s didn't deliver in a few areas: We had a recession, rampant inflation, and gasoline lines. I remember vividly as a kid the alternating odd and even gas days that enabled you to fill up your tank based upon your license plate number. The stock market produced negative growth, and we were saddled with record-high interest rates during the Carter administration. Mortgages averaged over 11% toward the tail end of the '70s and averaged as high as 17% in the early '80s.

The 1980s brought us into the age of money, which was everyone's scorecard. Movies like *Wall Street* were all the rage, and "greed was good," at least according to Michael Douglas's character, Gordon Gekko. "He who dies with the most toys wins" was a common axiom during the heyday of the '80s. The economic phase that began during this time period was a transition out of the industrial economy and into the service economy. It was less about manufacturing the next widget and more about intellectual capital and what value the space between your ears brought to the table.

As a general comment, it is important to note that as society goes from one economic cycle to the next, the attitude changes from appreciation to expectation. In other words, a business gets no points for doing what is expected, as those are considered table stakes—rather, they only lose points for not meeting expectations. The leadership style during this time quickly migrated away from command and control and into the *management as a science* mindset. The management consulting guru Peter Drucker dominated thought leadership on business management during this time. Drucker analyzed how humans organize across organizations and consulted with Japanese business leaders with regard to the rebuilding of their war-torn nation. Leaders in the '80s wove Drucker's ideas throughout the tapestry of their leadership styles.

The '90s brought about an era of cynicism as people realized that maybe they couldn't have it all. Due to rapid advances in technology, we were forced to do more in less time, making time itself the decade's primary commodity. Moving away from the '80s mindset of materialism, the '90s placed a greater emphasis on the experiential. Even though Starbucks was founded in the early '70s, its surging popularity in the '90s validated the advent of the experience economy. The experience economy recognized that mass customization was the way to increase market share and customer loyalty. Why else would you go out of the way to pay $5 for a cup of coffee at Starbucks when you could get it for $1.50 or less at 7-Eleven on your way to work? It's about how going to Starbucks makes you feel. You may feel hip, invigorated, accomplished, or part of something bigger than yourself by going to Starbucks for your cup of joe. Bottom line is Starbucks epitomized the experience economy. The type of leadership desired in the '90s was something termed the *un-leader*. Companies started instituting casual Fridays, and un-leaders organized and encouraged experiential outdoor bonding adventures between colleagues, such as rope courses, paintball games, and walking on hot coals. These things were designed to connote a more laid-back attitude from above in an effort to be hip and cool during the experience economy.

From the turn of the century to the present, we have been in the transformation economy. The societal attitude yearns for community more than ever before. In this age of social media, which is connectivity to the *n*th degree, we have become somewhat disenfranchised in the process. Relationships are not as robust as they were in times past. "Liking" something on Facebook or watching a YouTube video isn't the same as being there and immersed in someone's life experiences. This engagement is missing for many of us, leading to feelings of detachment.

Despite the proliferation of connectivity on the Internet, from email and texting to social media sites like Facebook, Instagram, Snapchat, Twitter, and LinkedIn, we are actually more disconnected than ever before—ironic, isn't it? In order to catch our attention as a society, the experiential has to morph into the transformational. With respect to your finances, how does what you are experiencing impact you directly, and what is its meaning to you and your life? Your experience needs to be contextualized and conceptualized for you, and the one person to do that is the *Money Navigator*.

Characteristics of Your Money Navigator Part I: Emotional Intelligence

In *Primal Leadership*, Daniel Goleman and his fellow authors Richard Boyatzis and Annie McKee bring the concept of emotional intelligence ("EI") to the forefront.[2] According to Goleman, EI indicates the capacity

---

2   D. Goleman, R.E. Boyatzis, and A. McKee, *Primal Leadership: Realizing the Power of Emotional Intelligence* (Boston: Harvard Business School Press, 2002).

we have for recognizing our own feelings and those of others and for managing emotions well in ourselves and in our relationships. To be clear, EI is not IQ, although they are related. Levels of EI are not predetermined by our DNA, nor do they only take form when we are little kids. Unlike IQ, which changes little after you are a teenager, EI is predominantly learned, and continues to develop as we go through life's experiences, according to Goleman. To be certain, your competence in EI continues to grow and expand as you age. This is good news for all of us because it means we can become more emotionally intelligent over time if we have the desire to change. A Money Navigator who recognizes the importance of being an emotionally intelligent leader to his clients is desired in today's culture.

EI comprises two overlying competencies of the Money Navigator: personal and social. Paying homage to Goleman's extensive work in EI, the Money Navigator's personal competence can be broken down into two subtopics: self-awareness and self-management, and social competence is broken down into social awareness and relationship management.

Let's first review the components of self-awareness. The first is *emotional self-awareness*, which refers to how the Money Navigator understands himself and his own emotions and their impact on others. This provides the Money Navigator with an ability to lead and make decisions with his gut, so to speak. This only comes from being aware of how he has, can, and will emotionally react in the future. The second is an *accurate self-assessment*, which refers to the Money Navigator being brutally honest with herself about her emotional strengths and weaknesses. This is not easily accomplished, because it forces the Money Navigator to be self-critical and to admit to being a flawed human being. At the same time, it is liberating because it enables the Money Navigator to improve and feel better about who she is becoming. The final component of the self-awareness category is *self-assurance*, which means the Money Navigator has to have a strong sense of self-worth and recognize and value his own competencies. This is where ego is allowed to rear its head and announce its particular areas of greatness.

Moving to the components of self-management, we first look at the topic of *self-control*. This refers to the Money Navigator regulating her negative emotions and keeping them in check. Being transparent with others is critical because it connotes truthfulness and veracity, which in turn naturally results in others trusting the Money Navigator. Earning your trust is vital if the Money Navigator expects to interact with you in a leadership capacity. The Money Navigator mustn't be so overly stringent and stuck in her ways that she cannot be adaptable to change, which of course is inevitable. Leaders need to be malleable and open to new ideas. Additionally, having a mindset of constant and consistent achievement is paramount when managing one's emotions, as is taking the initiative to look for and grasp potential opportunities. Leaders don't rest on their laurels; rather they are constantly challenging themselves and the status quo. Finally, being an optimist (but a realist) certainly doesn't hurt in keeping positive emotions at the forefront. An entire field has developed over the past twenty-five years around the topic of positive psychology. Shawn Achor's book *The Happiness Advantage*[3] (more on this in chapter 9) is a must-read about the power of positivity and happiness in our lives.

The next components we will review are those of *social awareness*. The first is empathy, which should be straightforward. This means the Money Navigator putting himself in the shoes of the person he is trying to actively understand: you, his client. Understanding organizational dynamics are also of importance, as often politics are involved, and it pays to be aware of and appreciate the decision matrices in play. A service component is critical so the Money Navigator is meeting your needs as well as the needs of his employees.

The last components we will review are related to *relationship management*. The first is inspiration, which means the Money Navigator has to have a compelling message and vision with the ability to motivate others to execute. Motivation is critical because without it, no action is taken and financial plans literally die on the shelf. Influence is vital, so it is imperative that the Money Navigator have an arsenal of convincing tactics available so people want to follow him. Developing others to become stronger with increased abilities should be a priority so they become more robust. When the Money Navigator helps by showing others how to become more effective or to improve their credentials, how can that not foster loyalty? Similarly, when change is necessary, being a catalyst to get others to buy in is important to successfully move in a new direction. This is where being bold in the face of fear can be a gravitational force and game changer. Inevitably there will be conflict, so managing disagreements is a

---

3   S. Achor, *The Happiness Advantage: The Seven Principles of Positive Psychology That Fuel Success and Performance at Work* (New York: Crown Publishing Group, 2010).

critical element. Everything will not always run smoothly in any endeavor, so the Money Navigator realizes that conflict is part of life and expects it. Finally, a collaborative teamwork approach results in positive outcomes, as everyone has in fact bought in to the new vision. The Money Navigator recognizes he is not a one-armed paper-hanger trying to do everything himself; rather he needs competent and enthusiastic people to assist him.

The abovementioned EI leadership competencies are easy to understand but difficult to implement in practice. Why should your financial advisor be a leader with strong EI skills? The answer is, in today's culture it takes an experienced EI leader who is self-aware and doesn't become easily rattled to pull off the majority of the aforementioned components of EI, which in turn provide you with a better FinLife®.

Characteristics of Your Money Navigator, Part 2: The Conative Style

Prior to learning about conative style, I took personality tests such as Myers-Briggs and various IQ tests. These tests measure the affective and cognitive, or the "feeling" and the "thinking" side of things. Affective tests measure our desires, motivations, attitudes, preferences, emotions, and values. Cognitive tests measure our IQ, skills, reasoning, knowledge, experience, and education. Conative tests, on the other hand, measure the "doing" aspects of who we are as human beings. In other words, conative tests, such as the Kolbe A Index (Kolbe), measure our drive, instincts, mental energy, innate force, and values.

The conative part of the brain is the least familiar; however, interestingly, it is the very essence of *who* we are and *how* we are.[4] Conative refers to our natural tendencies, our personal MO (modus operandi or method of operation) that results in our directed effort. The way you direct your effort stems from your unique conative style.

Our creative instincts provide us with the fuel that drives us to do one thing or another. Your particular and unique style exemplifies the core of creativity that resides inside of you. This core helps you to generate and utilize the limitless fuel derived from the creativity you have put into

---

4   K. Kolbe, *The Conative Connection: Uncovering the Link between Who You Are and How You Perform* (Reading: Addison-Wesley, 1990).

unique abilities related to your personal performance. Operating within your conative style puts you in what I call the efficiency wheelhouse where you never run out of gas. By operating in the efficiency wheelhouse you are better at solving problems and creating new ideas. It doesn't mean that you can't do things well outside of your zone; it simply means that you operate best when staying within the guardrails of your conative style.

The Money Navigator knows that "Fact Finders" gather and share information, while "Follow Thru" types sort and store information. "Quick Starts" deal with risk and uncertainty, while "Implementors" handle space and tangibles, according to Kolbe. The result of the Kolbe is based upon your scores, and your conative style is an amalgam of the two top scores which could be Fact Finder/Follow Thru, for example. Fact Finders/Follow Thrus are generally individuals who need a significant amount of information (fact-finding and data gathering) in order to move forward in their decision-making process. They also like to have systematized methods for following through on tasks. Conversely, a Quick Start/ Implementor is someone who is able to deal with risk quite effectively and works well with his hands, perhaps building things. My Kolbe A Index happens to be Fact Finder/Quick Start. This means that I require a lot of data, research, and information before moving forward, but once I have analyzed it, if appropriate, I am comfortable being able to move forward quite quickly and without hesitation.

So at this point you may be wondering what conative style has to do with financial planning. The better question may be what conative style has to do with leadership and more specifically the Money Navigator. It is imperative for the Money Navigator to be a leader as well as to understand her conative style. If she attempts to navigate outside of her efficiency wheelhouse of innate talent, then it can cause an exorbitant amount of stress. This can trickle down into her business by negatively impacting her staff, not to mention sapping her energy and stymieing her effectiveness and ability to serve you. Once the Money Navigator understands her conative style by taking the Kolbe A Index test, she is better equipped to assist you. The next step in the process is to have you complete the Kolbe A Index. If you would like to take the Kolbe, you can find it at www. kolbe.com. Once you have completed it, the Money Navigator can gain a basic understanding of your MO and how to adapt to it.

Let me provide you with a practical example of how this works. You already know that I am a Fact Finder/Quick Start, so let's say you are a Fact Finder/Follow Thru. If I were your Money Navigator, I would know that you might appreciate having me provide you with a considerable amount of data and research, but I would also know that your modus operandi (MO) dictates that you'd like a systematized process or framework to work within. I will specifically cater to that need and make sure that not only do you have the necessary quantity and quality of data, but that you also receive it in a systematized way and that the solution we derive is also thorough and structured. Conversely, the average financial advisor may be judging you purely on your personality (not your conative MO) and give you a couple of tables and charts and then expect you to make a quick decision on the issue at hand. This method completely misses your conative style, which saps your energy, your ability to follow along, and your desire to implement any of the advice she is trying to provide. In short, it does not instill trust or faith in the advisor's ability and hinders your ability to do effective financial planning. The Money Navigator does not make this mistake. To learn more about the differences between a Money Navigator and a regular financial planner, turn to chapter 8.

The Age of the Money Navigator

While the Money Navigator style of leadership can apply to a number of different fields, this book will dive into your financial Money Navigator: a CFP® professional. One important characteristic of the Money Navigator is his geographic proximity to you. National "experts" abound, but these talking heads and market prognosticators mostly just contribute to the information glut and resultant noise evident in today's culture. The Money Navigator operates within your community and, as such, can bring greater contextual awareness and clarity to the decisions you face. Remember: we are all facing choice overload. A Money Navigator assists you in making sense of it all by contextualizing the deluge of information into succinctness for your unique set of circumstances, which in turn *restores order*, provides you with *financial peace*, addresses your *specific quality of life issues*, and gives you a *safe harbor*.

In order to *restore order* when you're feeling overloaded and pressed for time, you need a way back toward your comfort zone—a place where you feel a greater sense of control. To get you there, your Money Navigator might ask, "What concerns you the most right now, financially?" This enables you to form an action plan and begin to implement it so you feel you are making progress toward your objectives and obtaining *financial peace*. The Money Navigator genuinely wants to know about your lifestyle objectives so he can get a sense of what "financial peace" means to you. He might ask you, "What would you like and specifically why?" Knowing the answer to this question permits the Money Navigator to help you prioritize your goals and objectives based upon your time frames and concerns so you achieve the *quality of life* you desire. Conversations that involve these advanced coaching questions run deep and are rich in content that provides the Money Navigator with the necessary ingredients to determine what the top priorities are for you based upon what you truly value. Ultimately the Money Navigator's goal is to be considered a *safe harbor* for you: He is able to contextualize the information overload so it makes sense and is applicable to your specific set of unique circumstances. He represents a safety zone where you can openly air out your hopes, dreams, and fears without pause, as he will listen intently without pretense or passing judgment.

Money Navigator Leadership Styles

When it comes to the Money Navigator, six primary leadership styles are evident in today's society. All of the styles have the ability to build resonance or something of significance or meaning. The first is the imaginative Money Navigator. This type of leader can motivate you to pursue your dreams through inspiration and focusing on your goals. The educating Money Navigator can assist you with achieving your individual goals by utilizing specific strategies or aligning your strengths and goals with the goals of a larger organization or team. The supportive Money Navigator builds rapport and accord by making personal connections between you and others. This type of leader is a morale builder, conflict solver, and great motivator during stressful times. The egalitarian Money Navigator listens to your opinions and attempts to build consensus by getting everyone involved so they all participate in the planning process. The demonstrative Money Navigator leads you by example by regularly achieving goals and objectives. Finally, an authoritative Money Navigator style can keep you calm even in times of crisis and turmoil. I would argue that the most effective and impactful Money Navigators exhibit characteristics of all of the aforementioned leadership styles. It depends upon the situation at hand, and having a larger toolbox of leadership tools enables the Money Navigator to not use a hammer all the time because in his eyes everything happens to look like a nail! As an aside, my personal leadership style is mostly a combination of imaginative, educating, and supportive, but there are times when I utilize the other three styles when the situation presents itself. What type of leadership style do you possess?

Your FinLife® is so much more than what's sitting in your bank account. It's also about what you want your life to be like and whether you have the resources to live it. If managed properly, your investments can lead you not only toward a secure retirement, but toward the lifestyle you want to achieve—you owe it to yourself to see what's possible. In this chapter, I've introduced you to both your FinLife® and to the type of leader most able to guide you through the challenges of smart money management: your Money Navigator. Now that you have a better understanding of the Money Navigator's characteristics when it comes to your finances, it's time to better understand your own. In the next chapter, I will introduce you to the differences between traditional and behavioral economics, and explain why the latter is much more important than you might think when it comes to determining the future of your FinLife®.

Chapter Takeaways

Cusp of Retirement

If you are within ten years of retirement, then this book can help you immensely. Due to the likelihood that these are your peak earning years, this is prime time for you to make necessary changes that can positively impact your FinLife® future. This is also the time not to make errors that could throw your retirement off track. You've heard the adage, there are no do-overs in life, so it's imperative to get it right the first time so you can live your Ideal FinLife® (more on this later). If your retirement is fast approaching, this book was written for you.

Already Retired

Recently I had an MRI done of my shoulder, and the orthopedic surgeon said I had torn my rotator cuff and needed surgery. I was told that the procedure required a rehab of approximately four to six months. Ugh! I decided to go to another orthopedist and found out that, although my rotator cuff was in fact torn, it was a micro-tear, and the real problem was my AC joint. I simply needed to have some physical therapy on my shoulder for six weeks, and the shoulder would be close to as good as new. Worst case, I'd need surgery on my AC joint, which would end up being only a four- to six-week rehab. Thank goodness for second opinions! If you are already in retirement, you have likely already given some thought to what you want your FinLife® to look like and what steps you might need to take to get there. A Money Navigator can give you the second opinion you need by reviewing your financial situation in a comprehensive fashion and providing you with a "diagnosis." You just might like what you hear, and if you don't, you are in no worse shape than before. Additionally, you may like some of the cutting-edge ideas and concepts you are presented specifically for your situation—that's your Money Navigator's leadership style in action.

Facing a Life Transition

So you are going to do it. You are getting married. Talk about facing a life transition! There are a bountiful number of self-help books on things to do to ensure a long, happy marriage. Most of these books discuss compatibility, relationships, logistics, and the emotions associated with marriage.

What are our feelings about religion? Do we both want children? Will we both have careers? Where will we live? How will we handle disagreements? How involved are our respective families in our daily lives? A smaller number of books review the financial side of marriage. Should our accounts be jointly titled? Should we each have our own checking accounts? What type of risk tolerance do we each have? What about life insurance? What are our long-term goals for retirement? How do we feel about debt? Do we each save regularly? What are our credit scores? What are our feelings about estate planning? Should we rent or buy a home? The list goes on and on.

Interestingly, virtually none of the books will review your conative styles and how they mesh or conflict with each other. Remember from earlier in this chapter that your conative style is your method of operation, or in essence, how you do things. In order for your marriage to be clicking on all cylinders, you both need to be operating in your efficiency wheelhouses, so I would recommend you each take the Kolbe A test to determine your conative styles—a Money Navigator can help you through this exercise and more. This will provide you with an amazing amount of clarity regarding how best to "do" things together. This matters in the relationship and in how you make financial decisions together. Remember: your FinLife® is so much more than finances!

CHAPTER 2

Traditional vs. Behavioral Finance

"Financial decision making is not necessarily about money. It is also about intangible motives like avoiding regret or achieving pride."
—Daniel Kahneman

Now that you know what a Money Navigator is and how they can help you better manage your FinLife®, let's take a look at what inspires our own financial decisions. In the mid-'80s there was a popular song called "Human" by The Human League. The song centers around our imperfect nature as humans and speaks to our inherent fallibility. Such an idea provides us with a perfect introduction into the world of behavioral finance. We are human, and whether we like it or not, we are all born and prone to make mistakes when it comes to our financial affairs. No one is immune to this phenomenon.

Behavioral finance may sound like an intimidating topic, but it's really not at all, because we all experience elements of behavioral finance every day. The concepts of behavioral finance will be pretty familiar to you, and you may experience a few "aha" moments as we progress through the book. In order to best manage your FinLife®, you must be aware of how your own behavior impacts the choices you make. This chapter will provide you with the tools you need to get started.

Overview of Traditional Finance vs. Behavioral Finance

Before diving into the specifics of behavioral finance, it is best to first discuss traditional finance in order to establish a baseline foundation for comparison. The two key components involved in finance are *investors* and the *market*.

- **Investors in Traditional Finance:**
  The standard theory of finance assumes that all investors are rational beings. Standard theory assumes that all information is considered and that its meaning is accurately interpreted. Some individuals may act irrationally or against predictions at times, but these individuals' actions don't really matter when they are considered as part of a large group.
- **Markets in Traditional Finance:**
  Where all known information is quickly incorporated into the market so it represents the true value of all stocks.

Traditional finance explains how investors *should* act based upon assumptions, models, and equations. Behavioral finance, on the other hand, integrates psychology, economics, and finance to explain how investors *actually* act. Behavioral finance helps us to better understand individuals' and groups' financial decision-making processes. If you understand how you may act in certain situations involving your finances, you will be better positioned to recognize this and therefore drive better financial outcomes for yourself and your family. This knowledge leads to self-reflective moments where you are able to identify a bias in your decision-making process and therefore can avoid a pitfall to which you otherwise may have fallen victim.

- **Investors in Behavioral Finance:**
  Based upon the historical actions of investors during market panics, investors are not always rational. Often you will act upon imperfect information. Our brains make errors where we exhibit a cognitive bias and thereby don't act completely objectively or rationally.
- **Markets in Behavioral Finance:**
  The markets are likely difficult to beat in the long run. However, in

the shorter term, there are inconsistencies, anomalies, and extremes.

Behavioral finance reminds us to stay aware of the fact that we can be victims of our own self-sabotaging behavior without even knowing it. In this book, as you explore behavioral finance, and more specifically decision traps, the goal is for you to become more self-aware of the many ways you can hinder your own FinLife® by making bad decisions. Gaining this self-awareness leads you toward better decision making, which ultimately impacts your FinLife® in a positive way.

Human Economic Behavior

Economics is often taught as a numbers science with mathematical formulae, charts, graphs, and supply and demand curves. Remember the "guns and butter" example your professor covered in Econ 101? This famous model explains the relationship between two goods that are both important for a given nation's growth and helps individuals consider optimal resource allocation. Economics is similar to behavioral finance in that human economic behavior is the study of how and why humans take either action or inaction based upon economic choices with which they are confronted.

To illustrate this, I'll share an experience I had recently at a Rotary breakfast meeting where I heard an impressive individual, with an MBA from an Ivy League school with practical experience in the financial services industry, conduct an interesting experiment. He asked for two volunteers from the audience. He asked them to stand and come to the front of the room with him. The speaker then proceeded to take out an envelope from his briefcase that contained ten brand-new, crisp one-dollar bills. He then told the participants that he was going to conduct an experiment with them. He gave all ten of the dollar bills to one of the volunteers and provided her with the following instructions. She had to divide the ten one-dollar bills in any way she desired between herself and the gentleman who had volunteered.

Sounds simple, right? Now here is the catch. The guest speaker told her that if the other volunteer didn't accept the amount she gave him, then neither of them would get any of the money. However, if the other volunteer accepted her chosen split of the funds, then they both would walk away with their respective share of the money. Pretty straightforward. Here's where it got interesting. The woman who had the power to divide the proceeds divided them equally, or $5 each. The other volunteer agreed, and the guest speaker let them keep the money as he promised he would do.

Then the speaker asked the man what amount of money he would have rejected. The man thought for a second and then sternly said $2, which on the surface seemed to make a lot of sense. I mean, if he received only $2 then that meant the woman volunteer decided to keep $8 for herself. That would have been downright unfair! But was it? Think about it for a second. If the man rejected the $2, was he being rational? Not necessarily, no. If he accepted any amount of money he was rational, but if he rejected any amount of money he was irrational. The reason this is the case is if he accepted any amount of money, he would be wealthier than he was prior to accepting the money. What the other volunteer was able to get from the experiment should have had absolutely no bearing whatsoever on his decision, but it did. He wasn't looking only at his newfound wealth, he was insisting on some sort of fairness between the woman and himself. Other factors were at work besides just the money he would receive.

Now, back to the woman volunteer. If she were acting completely rationally, she would have taken $9 for herself and given the man $1. She should have realized the man should have accepted $1 if he were being rational (because he would have improved his situation economically), but instead she also acted irrationally by citing fairness as the primary factor for splitting the proceeds. The bottom line: no one wants to feel cheated or slighted, so we may, as the famous saying goes, cut off our noses to spite our face!

Game Show Economics

Examples of the type of irrational human behavior I am talking about are everywhere. Recall the 1970s television game show, *Let's Make a Deal*, starring Monty Hall. Hall was the quizmaster and host of the show, which required audience members to dress up in silly costumes. Hall hosted many different kinds of games on the show, and one such game became the topic of quite a bit of controversy. According to *American Statistician*,[1] in 1975, Steve Selvin submitted a letter to the publication describing a game that was loosely based upon *Let's Make a Deal*. *Business Insider*[2] reported that the game reappeared in 1990, when Marilyn vos Savant, whose brainteasers have been a part of *Parade* magazine for decades, provided a hotly debated answer to a question a reader had posed to her. The question, based on Selvin's original letter, went something like this:

Let's say you are on a game show and you are shown three curtains. You are allowed to choose one of the curtains. You are told that there is a new car behind one of the curtains and there are goats behind each of the two others. So you decide to pick Curtain #1, and the host, who knows what is behind each curtain, opens another curtain, let's say Curtain #3, which reveals a goat. He tells you that you can switch to Curtain #2 or stay with Curtain #1. Is it advantageous to switch your choice of curtains?

Say what? This is truly a brainteaser, and intuitively something in your head tells you to calculate probabilities. You figure you've gotten it narrowed down to a 50/50 shot, right, since there is one goat and one car left? Your choice of Curtain #1 has a 50% chance of winning the car. You reason this is the case because initially you had a 33% chance or 1/3 chance of winning the car, and now your odds have improved. Sweet, you can already smell the new Corinthian leather and see Ricardo Montalban riding shotgun! But you are wrong. Your odds have not improved at all! You still only have a 33% chance to win the car because the result if you stay with Curtain #1 gives you a 1 in 3 chance of winning the car. Conversely, if you switch, you will have a 2 in 3 chance of winning the car. See the following matrix that Ms. vos Savant developed that supports this. In this example, it is assumed that you picked Curtain #1, but it holds true regardless of which curtain you pick to start the game. Also, as part

1   Steve Selvin, M. Bloxham, A. I. Khuri, Michael Moore, Rodney Coleman, G. Rex Bryce, James A. Hagans, Thomas C. Chalmers, E. A. Maxwell, and Gary N. Smith, *The American Statistician* 29, no. 1 (1975): 67–71.

2   Sara Silverstein and Matt Johnston, "The Monty Hall Problem: There's a Right Answer but Even Genius Math Geeks Get It Wrong," *Business Insider*, February 25, 2014, http://www.businessinsider.com/the-monty-hall-math-problem-2014-2.

of the game, keep in mind that the host will always reveal the goat behind one of the curtains you didn't select.

Behind Curtain #1	Behind Curtain #2	Behind Curtain #3	Result if stay with Curtain #1	Result if switch to Curtain offered
Car	Goat	Goat	**Wins the Car**	Wins a Goat
Goat	**Car**	Goat	Wins a Goat	**Wins the Car**
Goat	Goat	**Car**	Wins a Goat	**Wins the Car**

Table courtesy of Marilyn vos Savant, "Ask Marilyn," Parade *Magazine 25 (December 2, 1990.)*

Thousands of readers, including many PhDs, sent in letters disputing von Savant's correct answer. The point of the story is that *things are not always what they appear to be to our intuitive minds.* Sometimes you need to look at a problem from a different angle. By taking a fresh look and being self-aware about what's influencing your decision-making process, you give yourself a better chance to find financial success—and keep that success growing. A Money Navigator can help you refocus your lens.

Chapter Takeaways

Cusp of Retirement
The ten years or less leading up to your retirement are often when you receive the highest amount of income. It is not uncommon to invest a considerable amount of your income in order to fund your impending retirement. What can unfortunately occur is that you feel you need to make up for lost time and as a consequence succumb to self-imposed pressure to have your investments earn a high rate of return. This leads to taking on too much risk as a result of making an irrational decision about money that leads to a mismatch in investment choice compared to your risk tolerance. Remember that retirement is not a sprint; rather it is a marathon, and your asset allocation should be aligned with the next twenty-five years or more of your life that you will spend in retirement.

Already Retired
You are happily enjoying retirement and you have always invested a certain way. You buy blue chip, dividend-paying stocks and you may have ignored any other type of investment holdings. On the surface, there is nothing inherently wrong with this philosophy. On the other hand, you may be falling victim to the *Let's Make a Deal* problem, where you focus too much of your attention on one thing to the detriment of other legitimate possibilities and alternatives. The game show host made the show's contestants focus too much on winning the car and not on the actual odds involved of winning it. By buying only blue chip stocks you are myopically focusing on getting winning returns over time, but not on improving your odds for getting those types of returns via diversification, noncorrelation, and improved asset allocation. Before you invest, take a step back, inhale, exhale, and try to "win the car," because who wants a goat in retirement anyway?

Facing a Life Transition
You just inherited an amount of money that you know has clearly changed your life. I have witnessed clients receiving windfalls many times in my career. It could be an inheritance, life insurance proceeds, money from stock options or company stock, bonuses, etc. The common thread woven

through each of these events is the propensity of the recipient to lose a bit of self-control. Even though you likely know subconsciously that you shouldn't do so, you end up spending too much of your newfound wealth on something you really didn't want or need. Cars, real estate, consumer items, what have you, the point is your reactive brain triggers this response to the receipt of the money and acts without taking the longer term financial ramifications into account. By being consciously aware of behavioral finance and how it personally affects your decision making, you can stop your bad habits before they get built in the first place.

Navigating Your Decision Traps

"The brain is a wonderful organ; it starts working the moment you get up in the morning and does not stop working until you get to the office."

—Robert Frost

CHAPTER 3

How Humans Make Decisions

"It is in your moments of decision that your destiny is shaped."
—*Tony Robbins*

S ection I of this book provided you with an introduction to your FinLife® and explained how both you and your Money Navigator can positively influence the outcomes of your financial situation. The Money Navigator is well suited to today's culture, and his leadership style allows him to custom-create a plan that's right for you. You can affect your FinLife® for the better by simply being aware of the core concepts behind behavioral finance: Remember that no decision-making process happens in a bubble.

The aim of Section II is to build off of that introduction by outlining some of the core factors that influence your decision-making behaviors, clarifying some common stumbling blocks you might face when making those important financial decisions, and describing the ways in which both you and your Money Navigator can creatively and intentionally conquer the information overload that impedes the decision-making process.

In this chapter specifically, we'll dive a little deeper into the subtle elements of your life that factor into your decision making when it comes to finances. You may be surprised at all of the unconscious factors informing how and what you decide to do with your money.

Generational Dynamics

Which generation you were born into plays a large role when it comes to the decisions you make in your FinLife®. The Money Navigator understands that his client is a member of a generational class, which could be the millennials or gen Yers (1980–2000), the gen Xers (1965–1980), the baby boomers (1945–1965), or the matures (pre-1945). Each generation has its unique set of formative experiences, traits, and preferred methods of engagement.[1] Different generations have distinct views about products, politics, religion, careers, and many other areas in life. Generational dynamics are some of the most important factors that shape people's opinions and views. It is imperative that the Money Navigator has knowledge of the distinct generational differences that exist with respect to preferences, biases, and belief systems. This enables the Money Navigator to be more aware, effective, and impactful when interacting with an individual from a particular generational class. Let me briefly explain what I mean by discussing each generation's formative experiences and how that impacts the Money Navigator/client interface.

Millennials are a diverse group and have been raised in the digital world of personal computers, iPhones, iPads, social media, and exponential technology. Most use text messaging as their primary mode of communication. As a group they are active consumers, leading purchasers of technology who influence older generations' (think gen Xers and boomers who are the millennials' parents) spending habits. They are friends with their parents, unlike the relationships their mothers and fathers had with their own parents. Millennials can appear to be quite rushed as a group, and they prefer a pack environment. Conversely, they are also individualistic and have been emotionally impacted by events such as 9/11, mass shootings, and the '08 economic crash. This is an extremely influential group due to their familiarity with and inclination toward social media. Millennials also are cause oriented, and they appreciate a giving-back philosophy. They greatly value authenticity and like to feel connected. They provide feedback quickly, which leads to endorsements

---

1   Cam Marston wrote a great book about this very subject which I recommend, not so much for the "selling tactics" but to gain insight and perspective on the differences between generations. See C. Marston, *Generational Selling Tactics That Work: Quick and Dirty Secrets for Selling to Any Age Group* (Hoboken: Wiley and Sons, 2011).

or criticisms to and from their peer group. As a whole, their population of approximately eighty million is slightly greater than the boomers', and their spending power will exceed all generations that preceded them as they mature.

When working with millennials in a financial advisory capacity, the Money Navigator must recognize their individuality. Customized solutions are paramount with this group, as they like to be treated in a way that distinguishes their uniqueness. Cutting-edge tools and access to your business platform 365/24/7 are critical elements that the millennial client is looking for in an advisor. Cashless transactions, the ability to use credit/debit cards, and mobile payment methods are highly valued due to convenience. It is imperative to communicate, address, and solve any problems that arise with millennials, or an advisor risks a negative social media onslaught.

I am a gen Xer. Gen Xers grew up with television and are generally skeptical due to some of their formative experiences. They were privy to the Watergate scandal, gasoline shortages, the Iran hostage crisis, the *Challenger* crash, and the AIDS epidemic. Many gen Xers were latchkey kids in that they were products of their parents getting a divorce. As a result, single-parent families became more commonplace, and often kids had to fend for themselves. This led to skepticism about promises being kept, and this generation was the first that felt they might end up less well off than their parents, thereby making the American dream appear to be more of a mirage. In no hurry to enter the workforce or real life, many gen Xers postponed their careers and marriage for extended college and additional degrees or backpacking around Europe, for example.

Gen Xers would rather do business with an advisor first and *then* become his friend rather than the other way around. They don't want to be sold anything! Instead, they want to feel in control and that they have bought something after they have researched it, of course. Gen Xers are currently entering their peak spending years. In general, this is a well-educated and tech-savvy generation, so they can be extremely discerning about with whom they interact. Gen Xers have a general distrust for authority, and advisors need to prove themselves to them and earn their stripes, so to speak, before they are welcomed aboard. Confidentiality is paramount with this group, as they are guarded about personal information.

The Money Navigator knows that, although gen Xers can be a skeptical lot, once the gen Xer becomes a client, he is loyal. Gen Xers tend to do quite a bit of research before making decisions, and if they come into the Money Navigator's office for an initial meeting, it better be understood that they have conducted their own form of due diligence, as they tend to do their homework in advance. They are predisposed to planning as a result. This means that the Money Navigator's web presence should make the impression he wants it to make; otherwise he has lost the game before it has even started. The Money Navigator's social media pages better be fresh and filled with thought leadership, and his website must be engaging, up-to-date, and cutting edge. His conversations with gen Xers are direct and to the point, as they have high BS meters, so don't even attempt to spin a story with them. The Money Navigator realizes that gen Xers appreciate it if he respects their boundaries and gives them space to make decisions. The Money Navigator often wants to have a Plan B available because Gen Xers appreciate choice, but not choice overload of course.

Baby boomers are the wealthiest generation in United States history. Collectively, there are approximately seventy-six million boomers, and they are seriously thinking about retirement or are retired right now. They were born during a time of post–World War II optimism and economic prosperity. As a result, boomers feel that anything is possible in life. Boomers commonly challenge authority, as this is in their DNA. Think back to Vietnam War protests, and you will see footage of boomers expressing their constitutional rights. They grew up in an era of free love and experimentation, and they value experiential activities. Many boomers have smaller families than their parents as a result of getting married later in life, as a premium was placed upon obtaining additional education.

The Money Navigator knows that boomers are open to the sales process, meaning they are willing customers and appreciate hearing an advisor's company story and how it can help them. Unlike gen Xers, who would feel manipulated, boomers don't mind if you try to be their friend *first* and then conduct business. It is important that there is a degree of formality during the beginning stages of an advisory relationship—so the Money Navigator knows not to be overly casual at the onset of the engagement. Many boomers are now empty nesters with discretionary incomes. This money is often used to influence causes or initiatives for which the boomer is impassioned. When the Money Navigator engages with a boomer, she realizes that a big part of their identity is defined by their jobs, which oftentimes signify leadership roles, success, and status. Boomers have the propensity to wax nostalgic about how things used to be in culture and society. So being aware of their fondness of times past is important when interrelating with them.

The Money Navigator has found that boomers are realistically optimistic about life. They have a fondness for the past, tend to act younger than they are, and as a result are a pretty hip group, especially in the way they dress, the vacations they take, and the cars they drive. The Money Navigator makes sure that he communicates with boomers in a method with which they are comfortable, whether it's via email, telephone, regular mail, or texting. The Money Navigator knows that boomers can be stressed out because of their responsibility burdens at home, with work and often their parents, so the Money Navigator wants to make sure he doesn't create bottlenecks for them. Instead, the Money Navigator knows that boomers prefer customized solutions that provide them with control of their time, well-being, and finances. Being respectful of the opinions of the boomers' children is paramount, as many rely on their millennial and gen Xer offspring for assistance with technology, for example.

Matures were born prior to 1945, and they have the highest net worth of any generational group. The Great Depression made a significant impact on the lives of the matures. Matures value doing their perceived duty, pulling together as a nation, and they applied this to their work ethic, as many worked for the same employer for their entire careers. This can be summarized in one word: loyalty. They experienced the stock market crash of 1929, FDR's fireside chats, Pearl Harbor, World War II, the bombing of Japan, the Korean War, the Vietnam War, and the Cold War. As a result, matures respect authority and valued settling down and raising a family. Their source of news is predominantly the newspaper and television, and they are likely to vote in elections. Many matures desire to leave a legacy for their children and grandchildren.

The Money Navigator knows that matures value and appreciate quality. Prepackaged solutions are acceptable for this group if they come from a reputable source. Patriotism is highly valued, so an American flag flying in the office goes a long way and makes a strong impression. The Money Navigator knows that the matures are a wealthy group, but they are also conservative and cautious with their money. Once they become clients, they tend to be loyal, as they often get set in their ways. Showing respect to this generation is essential, and asking them how they prefer to interact (in person, mail, or telephone are the primary choices) is appreciated. The Money Navigator takes the time to educate his mature clients about difficult concepts as they appreciate learning a lot before rendering a decision.

Tying It All Together

The Money Navigator who is aware of and understands generational dynamics can speak your specific language as well as understand your biases and preferences. The Money Navigator realizes that your decision making, regardless of what generational group you belong to, is based on about 90% emotion and 10% logic. This enables the Money Navigator to add tremendous value in advising you on how to make smart decisions that impact your FinLife® without disregard for who you are from a generational perspective.

Birth Order

Birth Order by Dr. Kevin Leman is a book that provides a thorough study of the various characteristics and traits of first-born/only child, middle-born, and last-born children. Does birth order have anything to do with financial planning or investments? The answers may surprise you.

The Money Navigator is interested in birth order because it assists him with his relationship with you. Knowing whether you are a first, only, middle, or last-born child in the family provides the Money Navigator with a tremendous amount of information on how you may react to certain situations, your preferences, and in general terms, what your strengths and weaknesses may be. This information is not directly related to financial planning and investments, but I would argue that *the Money Navigator's number one job is to manage human behavior,* so he desires to seek to understand before he attempts to be understood. That way, the Money Navigator's message can be catered more appropriately and received more favorably by you. Another advantage to understanding birth order is the Money Navigator can help you become more aware of how the order of your birth and your resultant hardwiring may impact your decision making, which then leads to more clarity going forward. Let's now discuss the typical traits of each birth order.

First-Born or Only Child

The Money Navigator knows that first-borns typically are self-assured and confident individuals because they often have siblings to whom they have assumed a leadership role. This leads them to trust their own opinions and makes them unafraid to make decisions. Many times, especially if they are an only child, they may be self-centered from being treated by their parents as the center of the universe. At times they can be fearful or uncertain about trying new things. Perfectionist attitudes abound with first-borns, as they tend to do things right and leave no stone unturned as they attempt to do a thorough job. They can be highly self-critical as well as critical of others to a fault, and they are rarely satisfied. Ironically, perfectionists often procrastinate because they fear they cannot do a good enough job.

First-borns tend to be organized and have everything under control. They appear to be on top of things and are usually on time and on schedule. They may worry about order, rules, and processes and lack flexibility when it is needed. First-borns also display impatience with anyone who is disorganized or is not meticulous. Surprises or bumps in the road can upset the first-born. First-borns tend to be driven individuals who are ambitious, enterprising, energetic, and willing to pay the price of success. This can lead to their putting too much pressure on themselves and on those around them. List making is a common activity of a first-born. Goal setting is a by-product of making lists, and first-borns tend to reach their goals and get more done in a day than most. Planning is paramount for a first-born. This can lead to a feeling of becoming boxed in, overstressed, and too busy to see the forest for the trees, leading to missing out on prioritizing appropriately.

Known as logical, straight thinkers, first-borns can be counted on not to be compulsive or irrational. They may believe they are always right and not budge when it comes to their opinion. They can be stubborn to a fault if the opinions of others are intuitive. First-borns tend to be voracious readers—many reading two or more books per month. They accumulate and store information and can recall facts quite easily. Problem solving is a strong suit for first-borns. Many times first-borns spend too much time gathering data when other issues or problems are more pressing. Sometimes they can be too serious and miss the humor in situations where humor can go a long way.

Middle-Born

Middle-born children grew up feeling squeezed and rootless. They naturally learned not to be spoiled, and they were not the center of the universe in their parents' eyes. Often middle-borns are the rebellious types and feel they simply don't fit in. They have reasonable expectation levels because, quite frankly, life has not always been fair to them; they haven't been spoiled and are more realistic and less jaded. Sometimes, because they feel they have been treated unfairly or have gotten a raw deal, they can be suspicious, cynical, and even bitter about people, issues, or ideas. Middle-borns are socially active folks, and relationships are important to them. When they make friends, they tend to keep them long term and remain loyal. Sometimes friends can be too important, and not offending them may cloud judgment in key decision-making situations.

Middle-borns are independent thinkers for the most part, and they are willing to do things differently. It is not uncommon for them to take risks and have a go at it on their own. This can lead to being stubborn or bullheaded and simply unwilling to be cooperative. Conversely, middle-borns can be compromising and know how to get along with others well. Professional mediators and negotiators are commonly middle-borns because they have experience in handling disagreements and disputes as they grew up. They have the empathy necessary to see both sides of an argument. This can result in peace being the goal at any price, and others, astute in recognizing this, can take advantage of this situation.

Diplomacy is a strength of middle-borns. They are natural peacemakers, are willing to work things out, and are great at seeing issues from both vantage points. They hate confrontation and often choose not to share their real opinions and feelings. The Money Navigator knows that this leads to middle-borns exhibiting secretive behavior, whereas as a result they can be trusted with sensitive information. Many times, however, they can fail to admit when they need help, because it is far too embarrassing to them.

Last-Born

Last-borns tend to be charming, likable, fun to be around, and easy to talk to. They can, however, be manipulative and even a little "out there" or considered flaky. They oftentimes sensationalize things and are categorized as being slick and a bit unbelievable. Last-borns are people-oriented, read others well, and generally know how to relate and work well one-on-one or in small groups. They gravitate toward social settings like moths to a streetlight. They may come across as undisciplined and prone to talk too much and for too long. Often they can't walk the walk or talk the talk, as they are the kind who talks a good game but when the pressure is on, cannot produce. Tenacity is a common characteristic of last-borns, as they will keep on coming with tireless persistence and will not take no for an answer. This makes last-borns ideal cold-calling salespeople, an interesting side note. A weakness is the fact that in their quest to push it to the limit, they may push too hard because they only see things through their unique lens.

The Money Navigator knows that last-borns are usually affectionate and engaging individuals. They are caring, lovable, and generally want to help. As much as they like to get strokes for good deeds, they also like to give them out, too. Gullibility is often associated with last-borns, so they may be taken advantage of, and they make decisions too much based upon their feelings and not enough on fact and cogitation. Last-borns are characteristically uncomplicated people and appear relaxed, genuine, authentic, and trustworthy with no hidden agendas. "What you see is what you get" comes to mind when describing a last-born. This may lead to an appearance of absent-mindedness and being called an airhead! Attention seeking and entertaining is another trait of the last-born. These folks know how to get noticed. This may lead to an appearance of self-centeredness and a perceived egotistical temperament. Often last-borns can be classified as being spoiled and impatient.

Making Sense of It All

So did any of the above resonate with you? I know it did with me when I read it for the first time. I am a first-born, and I had many "aha" moments as I learned more about my innate strengths and weaknesses related to my birth order. You may not exhibit all of the characteristics in the particular section applicable to your birth order listed above. The idea is to provide you with a general framework to show you the dominant traits you may possess. In reality, your traits may meld so that you have some characteristics of all three birth orders.

The primary purpose of the previous section was to provide you with an overview of the birth order phenomenon so you can potentially understand yourself and those around you better as well as synthesize how this is important information for the Money Navigator to understand when working with you. Part of your decision-making process is undoubtedly influenced by your order of birth, and having a Money Navigator who understands that fact can only improve your choices and how they impact you financially going forward.

Your Money Mind®

When it comes to thinking about spending and saving money, the majority of us fall into one of three types. These types make up your Money Mind®. Your Money Mind® plays an integral role in the way you make financial decisions. It speaks to your deepest intentions and motivations— things that push you forward in your FinLife®. Becoming more aware of your Money Mind® will allow you to use it to your advantage.

At my firm in particular, the Money Navigator uses some interactive and engaging exercises with you that help you better understand who you are from a financial perspective, or better put, help you to determine your Money Mind®. He also uses the Honest Conversations® (www.unitedcp. com/honest-conversations) exercise to assist him in eliciting what it is that you truly value in your FinLife®.

The Find Your Money Mind® analyzer is a fun, interactive exercise that helps to provide you with perspective on the ways you feel about money and how your innate biases (we all have them) impact your decision making. This is not meant to call you out on your flaws; rather it is designed to help you determine if you have made financial decisions that you have regretted, only to repeat those same mistakes again, and what you can do about it. Do you get intimidated by even modest financial obligations or do you avoid conversations about money altogether? The exercise is designed so you can better understand yourself, your Money Mind®, and become more comfortable with and communicate more openly about your current and future financial situation. After you answer about seven questions, the results are tabulated and it is determined that you are either a Fear-, Commitment-, or Happiness-focused Money Mind®.[2]

If you are a fear-focused Money Mind®, you are concerned about being

---

2 Joe Duran, CFA, wrote the best-selling book *The Money Code*, which discusses our company's Money Mind® exercise in detail. I highly recommend picking up a copy at my company's website, www.unitedcp.com/the-money-code.

the *protector*, and you seek safety and security. It is difficult for Fear Money Minds® to find genuine peace of mind, and you are cautious and deliberate in your decision making. Big decisions can create a significant amount of anxiety for you, and you will delay enjoyment for the sake of feeling protected. The Money Navigator can help you when you are making financial decisions to ensure that your fear is not inhibiting sound judgment. He can help you to understand that some risk is necessary in order to financially succeed in life. Finally, the Money Navigator can provide you with a methodology (via the Money Mind® exercise at www.unitedcp.com/money-mind-analyzer) to help you determine if your fears are unreasonable and bring clarity to the situation.

If you are a commitment-focused Money Mind®, it is highly likely that you are a *giver* and want to help others. As a matter of fact, you never feel like you give enough and are extremely concerned about other's perspectives, so much so that you likely overemphasize others' opinions about money. You tend to make personal sacrifices to your own detriment, whereby you often neglect your own FinLife®. Generally, you are trusting of others who may lead you astray or manipulate you, since you tend to place too much weight on other's opinions. The Money Navigator can help you to ensure that your desire to please others is not inhibiting sound financial judgment and that you should take personal responsibility for your own financial well-being. A big part of this process is having you clearly articulate what you feel are your perceived FinLife® needs.

The happiness-focused Money Mind® seeks satisfaction and can be categorized as a *pleasure seeker*. If you are in this category, you simply feel like you never have enough time or money to do all of the things in life that you deem are important to you. You tend to make financial decisions quite quickly and don't consider their ramifications, as your primary goal is to maximize the benefit from your resources. This instant gratification bent leads you to underestimate or completely neglect or ignore future risks that may exist in your FinLife®. The Money Navigator can help be your impulse control governor, so to speak, by helping you to not make decisions on a whim based upon your pleasure-seeking approach. He can also bring reality to the forefront by providing you with perspective on your overly optimistic outlook. The Money Navigator can help you to slow down and be more objective when you are evaluating various alternatives that involve money.

What Does It All Mean?

The three Money Minds®—Fear, Commitment, and Happiness—each have their pros and cons. The main point of the exercise is self-awareness so you can examine the decisions you have made and understand why you have made them. By being more cognizant of who you are and your innate biases toward money, you become better equipped to make smarter decisions that impact your FinLife®. The Money Navigator who understands the Money Mind® analyzer is an invaluable resource for someone who does not have the do-it-yourself (DIY) mentality. This person is exceptionally busy with their work, home, and leisure pursuits, and highly values independent professional FinLife® management advice.

Chapter Takeaways

Cusp of Retirement

"What brings you here today?" What an amazing question. There are so many possible answers, yet the common theme the Money Navigator hears woven through the thread of the conversations is you are concerned about being able to retire on your time frame and on your terms. Bar none, that is the number one answer the Money Navigator receives! If you are less than ten years out from retirement, you are thinking this very thought right now as you read this text. In order to quell your concerns, you must take the time to understand the factors determining your decision-making outlook. What's your Money Mind®, and how is it working for or against your goals? How about your birth order? Now is the time to assess your possible weaknesses and tweak accordingly while you still have a few years ahead of you before retirement to make adjustments as needed.

Already Retired

If you are already retired, you likely are a boomer or from the mature generation. Sure, you could certainly be a retired gen Xer or perhaps even a retired millennial, but suffice it to say that the majority of retirees are boomers and matures at this point in time.

So if you are a boomer, for example, how do you want your Money Navigator to interact with you, and ideally what is the experience like when you work with him? If you are like most boomers, you likely are somewhat open to a friendly sales process initially in order to acquire background about an advisor and the services that he provides. You also want your status and success to be acknowledged by the Money Navigator but not in an in-your-face way, as subtlety commands a premium. As your relationship progresses, you appreciate the fact that your Money Navigator creates tailor-made ideas and solutions for your particular needs, not off-the-shelf mass customized products and services. You feel like he really "gets" you as a result. He even incorporates your kids into the mix if you are welcoming to the idea.

If you are a mature, you value loyalty, education, tradition, and all that it stands for. In the context of your Money Navigator, loyalty means trustworthiness. Trust is earned over time, and the Money Navigator embarks on a journey of trust with you from Day 1. Education is valued by matures, so the Money Navigator goes out of his way to ensure that he educates you on all facets of FinLife®. Finally, tradition becomes an institution for matures, and the Money Navigator acknowledges the beliefs and value systems that you have incorporated into your daily life. From the type of car you drive to where you live, tradition is evident everywhere.

Facing a Life Transition

Your FinLife® is often affected not only by your own life transitions, but also by your family's. Let's say your only daughter is getting married. You've saved up some money to pay for her wedding, but you and your partner have vastly different approaches and priorities when it comes to making decisions. A fear-focused Money Mind®, perhaps you are unwilling to go over budget at any cost. Your partner, however, is a happiness-focused Money Mind® and believes that this special occasion warrants more flexible spending. We all know that philosophical differences about money and spending are the root cause of many relationship issues, and this is no relationship guidebook. However, framing your spending decisions in terms of your Money Mind® can give two partners some space to discuss trade-offs, compromises, and decisions in a way that doesn't require finger pointing.

CHAPTER 4

The Decision Traps

*"Peter Lynch ran the Fidelity Magellan fund from 1977 to
1990, delivering an astonishing 29% average annual return
during his tenure. Despite his remarkable performance while
running the fund, Fidelity found that the average investor actually
lost money during his thirteen-year tenure."*
—Matt Driscoll

A
t its core, this book aims to help you understand your inherent
biases and, as a result, become more self-aware of how certain
unconscious biases and "decision traps" impact your financial
well-being. Ideally this resultant self-awareness can lead you
toward more positive changes and away from what is known as self-sabotaging behavior. This chapter provides an in-depth view of the decision
traps you may fall victim to and clarifies how a CFP® professional can
help you avoid these traps for greater financial well-being. Keep in mind
as you read through that solutions to these traps are discussed in a later
chapter (the one about FIAs). By being conscious of these traps, you can
increase the odds of avoiding them and keeping yourself moving in the
right direction. A Money Navigator knows these traps well, and can help
you from falling prey to the type of thinking they encourage.

Common Investor Decision Traps

One important step in the process of becoming more self-aware is learning
how to distinguish the differences between two common decision-making

methods: your *intuition* and *reflection*. Intuition is the gut feeling you have about a decision that you can act upon quickly and without much thought. Your intuition is informed by a series of mental shortcuts called heuristics, which reduce complex problems down into oversimplified solutions. As a result, we regularly make errors in judgment. This happens to all of us! Reflection, on the other hand, requires more gray matter and forces you to exert effort and cogitate in order to formulate rational decisions. Whereas heuristics allow for a quick solution to be determined and acted upon, reflection takes time and thought. Depending upon which method of decision making is utilized in a given situation, the results often vary greatly.

People tend to view the world, and more applicably their investment decisions, through their own unique lens using intuition and heuristics. This helps to reduce the strain on our brains when predicting values and probabilities during the decision-making process. However, when you use heuristics your biases take over, objectivity is thrown out the window, rules of thumb result, and subjectivity rears its head—ultimately causing you to lose out on possible gains.

Before we talk about other important issues relevant to financial decision making, I ask you to review the various traps outlined here. You may not recognize just one; you may have two, three, or more traps you regularly fall into. It's not about judging your past behavior; it's about understanding it and being self-reflective of what you have done and how you have done it.

Opinion Trap	Expert Trap
Internal Conflict Trap	Silo Trap
Prudence Trap	Myopia Trap
Confirming Evidence Trap	Overconfident Forecast Trap
Loss Recognition Trap	Probability Trap
Rearview Mirror Trap	Self-Sabotage Trap
Gambler's Trap	"As Is" Trap
Disproportionate Pain Trap	

The Opinion Trap

"To reach port, we must sail—sail, not tie anchor—sail, not drift."
—*Franklin D. Roosevelt*

You fall victim to the opinion trap when you anchor yourself at an initial position while making a prediction and then refuse to modify your reference point and opinion from there. You can fall victim to this trap when you evaluate many possible outcomes of an investment over the long term. You may have the opinion that the investment will provide a certain rate of return because of your research and you have anchored yourself there—this is your firm belief. It's much more difficult to change your beliefs than it is to simply keep believing what you've always thought to be true. However, as time goes on, if you fail to adjust your expected return when the risk of the investment has increased, you could be more and more disappointed with the result because the range of possible returns has increased and changed. Portfolio drawdown risk (maximum possible annual decline in investment value) is amplified as a result. Staying stuck in your opinion blinds you to the changes that are happening and does not allow you to make a necessary tweak or change to avoid a negative consequence.

The Internal Conflict Trap

"Peace is not the absence of conflict, but the ability to cope with it."
—*Mahatma Gandhi*

The internal conflict trap results when you get psychologically stressed because you consider two conflicting ideas simultaneously, or when something you previously believed is suddenly challenged by new information. A practical example of this is when you buy a new car and you think you got an amazing deal on it. You walk next door and excitedly tell your neighbor about it only to have your neighbor tell you that they just received a mailing for a special deal on a comparable competitive model that also includes free maintenance. How does this make you feel? You just bought a new car and felt that you received the best deal and now you have received conflicting information to the contrary. Your neighbor got essentially the same car plus free maintenance. "This is not fair," you say to yourself. So what do you then do? Do you go to Edmunds.com and start researching all over again? Do you make peace with the situation by telling yourself that you are still okay with your purchase even though you didn't receive free maintenance? Or do you think about going online to research the deal but instead decide not to because you are afraid to confirm that you made a mistake? To avoid mental discomfort you may justify your purchase to yourself and others that the car you bought was the better one, regardless of new information to the contrary. You persevere in the face of conflicting information and insist that you were correct.

People exhibiting cognitive dissonance characteristics often also show signs of selective attention. But have you heard about the invisible gorilla? I first heard about the invisible gorilla when I was taking a postdoctoral professional certification course entitled "Biases in Decision Making" from Stanford University's Center for Professional Development. Christopher Chabris and Daniel Simmons recorded a short video of two teams passing basketballs to each other. The task of the viewer is to count the number of passes that the team wearing white uniforms makes during the video. Meanwhile, the team wearing black uniforms is also passing a basketball and weaving in and out of the white uniform team members as they pass a separate basketball. At the end of the video, the viewer is asked how many times the team wearing white passed the basketball. The answer is fifteen. Then on the screen "But did you see the gorilla?" appears. What in the world are they talking about, the viewer might ask? After rewinding the video and watching it again, the viewer will distinctly see a person in a gorilla costume appear on the screen, beat his chest, and then run off in the other direction.

The test shows that humans can fall victim to selective attention, or seeing something other than reality, based upon preconceived notions or ideas. We see what we want to see or what we are focused on, and we can lose sight of what we really need to see instead.

The Prudence Trap

"Affairs are easier of entrance than of exit; and it is common prudence to see our way out before we venture in."

—*Aesop*

You have certain ideas about how the world and the financial markets work. It is common for you to be prudent and hold on to those ideas even in the face of new information or evidence to the contrary. However, this may lead you to place *more* weight on your existing beliefs and *less* on new information. It takes more mental bandwidth for you to process new information. You have to stretch your gray matter in order to evaluate the data and render a decision, and who wants to do that when you think you have all of the necessary information already? If you fall victim to this trap, you are likely to react to new data at a slow pace, which could further hinder the performance of your investment portfolio. Change is hard for most humans, and changing opinions may be hardest of all. Refusing to take in new information and process what it means to you can leave you stuck.

The Confirming Evidence Trap

"Facts are stubborn things; and whatever may be our wishes, our inclinations, or the dictates of our passions, they cannot alter the state of facts and evidence."
—*John Adams*

You are more likely to favor information that confirms your beliefs or ideas and devalue anything that contradicts them. This is because you tend to remember things selectively and interpret data in a biased way. When you look for validation and ignore information that may contradict what you believe, you set yourself up for self-sabotage. You probably have paid closer attention to a political candidate on TV that is espousing your beliefs than to one who is not. In fact, you likely have discounted or downplayed the opposing candidate's points of view because you feel that what he or she is saying could not possibly be correct or worth listening to. You also overemphasize events if they substantiate your viewpoint and ignore those that don't match up with your beliefs. A common example of the confirming evidence trap is employees investing in company stock. Individuals often overinvest in company stock plans due to familiarity and loyalty or simply peer or superior pressure. This obviously presents a problem for them if the company's stock drops significantly.

The Loss Recognition Trap

"Everyone lives by selling something."

—*Robert Louis Stevenson*

You won't sell your stock in ABC Corporation because it has dropped considerably in value, but you sold XYZ Company because you made some money on the stock. You are less willing to recognize losses (and you would have to do this if you sold ABC Corp), but you are more inclined to recognize gains.[1] At its core this doesn't make sense because the future performance of ABC Corp is completely unrelated to its purchase price. Think about it: you should really want to *sell* ABC to take advantage of tax loss harvesting—the idea of taking a loss to offset other gains, or in this case gains on XYZ stock, for example. As humans, we do not like to dispose of things that we possess and with which we have become familiar, as we form an emotional attachment that is difficult to break.

The Rearview Mirror Trap

"In hindsight, if I could go back in time and relay a message to my younger self, I would tell him to work on his timekeeping, and that the job of a drummer is not to be the one that gets noticed the most on stage, or to be the fastest, or the loudest. Above all, it is to be the timekeeper."

—*Taylor Hawkins, of the Foo Fighters*

You and your friend just watched a horse race and the horse you bet on, the favorite, lost to another horse (the one your friend wagered on, of course) that had a low chance of winning. After the race, you say to your friend that you "knew it all along" that it wasn't your horse's day and you knew you should have bet on your friend's horse. The fascinating part is you end up believing that the event was predictable and that you knew it, when in fact it was not. You think this because it is easier for humans to grasp and understand an event that has *actually* happened than to try to think of all of the possible things that *could* have occurred. This is why

---

1   Daniel Kahneman, *Thinking, Fast and Slow* (New York: Farrar, Straus and Giroux, 2011).

hindsight is said to be 20/20; you have perfect vision when looking in the rearview mirror. Unfortunately, you may not realize the distortions occurring in the mirror when looking behind!

The Gambler's Trap

"A journey is like a marriage. The certain way to be wrong is to think you can control it."

—*John Steinbeck*

You think you can control events when, in fact, you have no influence on the event at all. Gamblers often exhibit this bias. Watch a player at the craps table in a casino ask the crowd for silence because he needs to "roll a small number" or when he blows on the dice to "persuade" them to cooperate. Or observe a roulette table and ask a player why they play certain numbers. One may hear "the number six is my daughter's birthday" or "the 24th is our anniversary." Clearly, craps and roulette are games of chance, and control is nonexistent. Additionally, some people who buy lottery tickets exhibit the illusion of control when they have to play "their numbers," as opposed to buying a computer-generated ticket, as if this improves their chances of winning, when it clearly does not. Stress and competition increase the illusion of control, and this is an important point to keep in mind as you move forward with any investment or financial decision.

The Disproportionate Pain Trap

"Evolutionary psychologists suggest that humans experienced evolutionary benefits from brain developments that included aversion to loss and risk, and from instincts for cooperation that help strengthen communities."

—*Ben Bernanke*

The basic premise of loss aversion is that the good feelings you have after winning a sum of money, say $200 at a casino, will be less than the emotional pain you feel if you lose $100. In other words, even though in this example you lost half of what you won, the emotions you feel in both of the cases do not equate, nor is the emotional pain less because the dollar amount lost is lower. The truth is, you are more upset emotionally about losing $100 than you are happy for winning twice as much money! How can this be? The answer is that most individuals are loss averse and simply do not want to experience the pain of losses.[2] For example, let's say you purchased two stocks a few years ago, each for $150/share. Stock A has doubled in value during this time to $300/share, and Stock B's value has been cut in half, or gone down to $75/share. Even though if you sold your holdings you could double your money on Stock A and will have grown your overall money by 25% ($375 − $300 divided by your initial investment of $300), you don't want to sell Stock B. You rationalize this by saying to yourself that "it will come back; it just needs more time." The fact is, as humans we seek pleasure, but we also disproportionately seek to avoid pain.

The Expert Trap

"I am not antimedia at all. But the media, the news anywhere in the world, is based on drama."

—Peter Jackson

Don't lose sight of what sells magazines, newspapers, and gets eyeballs on the screen (television, tablet, computer, or smartphone). Sensational news sells, and in the financial industry, what sells best is the *crisis du jour*. When you sit down to the dinner table and turn on the financial news and hear that it is different this time, the sky is truly falling and we are all doomed, how do you respond? Many individuals are unduly influenced by the media and will make irrational financial decisions based upon what they hear from the "expert" on the tube or in a blog or magazine that they read. The thing to be aware of here is that the pundits have no idea how/if what they are saying applies to you personally. Let's say that it is being reported in the news that everyone should be investing in gold because inflation is predicted to spike by 1% in the next quarter. First of all, economic forecasts are notoriously inaccurate, and second of all, what impact does inflation increasing by 1% have to do with your overall ability to achieve your financial goals? Should you invest in gold? Maybe, but also maybe

---

2   Kahneman, *Thinking, Fast and Slow.*

not. Your Money Navigator should be consulted when you are thinking of making knee-jerk reactions to market news, as he can contextualize what this means to you, if anything at all, and as a result, what actions to take or not take.

The Silo Trap

"I worked in accounting for two and a half years, realized that wasn't what I wanted to do with the rest of my life, and decided I was just going to give comedy a try."

—*Bob Newhart*

This trap happens when, in your mind, you separate accounts into different buckets or silos. You do this by saying to yourself, "This is my slush fund," this account is my "vacation fund," and this account is for "retirement"—it's a game of mental accounting. You then pay attention to each account individually while not paying close attention to your overall portfolio and how each piece interrelates. This myopia can hinder your performance because you are unfocused on the big picture and the fact that money is money regardless of within which account it resides. One of the shortcomings of mental accounting is you often end up having an overlap of similar holdings or asset classes across accounts and therefore become underdiversified. This can put your portfolio at risk and make it perform suboptimally.

The Myopia Trap

"A journalist is supposed to present an unbiased portrait of an event, a view devoid of intimate emotion. This is impossible, of course. The framing of an image, by its very composition, represents a choice. The photographer chooses what to show and what to exclude."

—*Alexandra Kerry*

Depending upon what type of frame is placed around a work of art, your impression of that painting will likely be different. Let's face it, if you are in the Louvre staring at a Rembrandt in an Italian Renaissance frame versus a twentieth-century streamlined frame, your feelings about the same painting may be significantly different. Similarly, the concept of narrow framing may influence your feelings about a decision depending upon the context in which the choices are presented. For example, if markets become volatile, then you can myopically focus on negative volatility. Various levels of volatility can connote the riskiness of different types of investments. The more volatile the investment, the greater the expected return over the long term, but the more unpredictable the return in the short term. By narrowly framing the situation and focusing on negative short-term volatility, you can hinder your long-term performance by selling the investment in a panic.

The Overconfident Forecast Trap

"Courage is willingness to take the risk once you know the odds. Optimistic overconfidence means you are taking the risk because you don't know the odds. It's a big difference."

—*Daniel Kahneman*

You may have unwarranted self-confidence in your decision-making capabilities, judgment, and reasoning. Many individuals think they are smarter than they actually are and that they have all the information they need to make a decision; this is often due to a mistaken belief that one is in possession of a knowledge advantage. An example that resonates with many people is what occurred in the mid-2000s leading up to the real estate crash in 2008 and 2009. Real estate investment "experts" popped up overnight, and many of these self-proclaimed gurus bought multiple rental properties with little, if any, money down, or worse yet, used cash-out refinancing to buy new homes. As a result, they became highly leveraged as they took on more mortgage debt than was reasonable. The thought was that everything would continue to go on forever with property values continuing to escalate. When the euphemistic game of musical chairs ended, these individuals had nowhere to sit down. As is all too familiar, many of these individuals underestimated their downside risk and lost their proverbial shirts in the crash due to the overconfident forecast trap.

The Probability Trap

"The United States can pay any debt it has because we can always print money to do that. So there is zero probability of default."

—Alan Greenspan

The Probability Trap is sometimes exhibited by individuals when they are confronting situations regarding probabilities. For example, suppose person A, John, is introverted and he either belongs to group B (pension actuaries) or group C (salesmen). Heuristically, how do individuals evaluate to which group John likely belongs? Most people would attempt to determine the probability that John is an actuary by the degree to which A is *representative* of B or C. Clearly, it appears that John's introverted nature appears to align more closely with, and therefore be *representative* of, pension actuaries. In the process of determining that John appears to be a pension actuary, individuals often neglect base rates—in this case, the fact that there are far more salesmen than pension actuaries. Similarly, investors can misdiagnose the risk of an investment by thinking that the investment is representative of something that it is not. This is termed an "illusion of validity," as coined by Tversky & Kahneman, as a risk-averse investor may incorrectly think that a high-yield bond fund is a conservative instrument due to the investor associating the fund with highly rated bonds, instruments that traditionally connote conservatism.[3] Another example: Individuals may seek out yesterday's winning funds and buy them with the hopes that they will do well again in the future. This is often simply not the case.

The Self-Sabotage Trap

"As a tennis player you can win and you can lose, and you have to be ready for both. I practiced self-control as a kid, but as you get older they both—winning and losing—get easier."

—Rafael Nadal

---

3   Daniel Kahneman and Amos Tversky, "On the Psychology of Prediction," *Psychological Review* 80, no. 4 (1973): 237–251.

We've all seen the television commercial of a well-known financial services company about saving for retirement. The ads are particularly clever and the "built-in sauce rack" spot may be the best one. The premise of the commercials is that we all have regular money and orange money. Our orange money is what we need to save now for retirement tomorrow. The grill shopper's self-control is on display as he contemplates the fancy new grill with or without the expensive built-in sauce rack, which will undoubtedly cut into his orange money if he indulges himself.

Another example is an individual who is overweight and trying to lose pounds because he knows that his doctor told him that it was necessary for his physical well-being. Although he has a check-up coming up soon and still needs to shed some weight prior to the physical exam, he succumbs to self-sabotage by eating a gallon of ice cream. This provides him with temporary satisfaction, but his lack of self-discipline in the short term can hinder his health long term.

Investing in general is similar to the examples mentioned above in that consuming today in lieu of saving for tomorrow can cause irreparable harm to one's retirement planning.

The "As Is" Trap

"I don't accept the status quo, but I do accept MasterCard, Visa, or American Express."

—*Stephen Colbert*

Why change? Everything is fine just like it is. How often have you heard those words or said similar ones yourself? If there is a change proposed from the baseline or status quo, you often perceive it as a loss. As we discussed earlier, most of us are loss averse, so the status quo can become an anchor to progress or change. Additionally, maintaining the status quo can be explained by the concept of regret avoidance, or fear of making a decision we might regret later. Investors often take no action and may continue to hold inappropriate investment vehicles as compared to their risk tolerance.

Invest*ment* Returns vs. Invest*or* Returns

A CFP® professional who is a Money Navigator may help you to neutralize many of your natural human tendencies which lead to poor *investor* returns. Notice that I did not say *investment* returns, because there is a distinct difference between the two. Investor return is how your portfolio performs over a specific period of time, with your biases and actions taken into account. Investment return is the actual return earned by an investment vehicle over a particular period of time. Historically, average investor returns are significantly less than investment returns. Investors typically suffer from poor timing decisions and inadequate planning. Carl Richards appropriately calls the difference between investment returns and investor returns the "Behavior Gap."[4]

Interestingly, most investors understand the concept of investment diversification, but then deviate from being diversified because they place too large of an emphasis on past performance, herd mentality, and chasing returns—in other words, they fall victim to one or more of the above decision traps. This behavior manifests itself by investors selling their investments at the wrong times, often in reaction to bad economic news and market turmoil. Many studies have been conducted on this topic, and Dalbar has published an annual report called the "Quantitative Analysis of Investor Behavior" on how average investors continually underperform their investments.[5] I researched this topic during my master's in finance studies, and my PhD dissertation included the subject of comparing invest*ment* versus invest*or* returns.

The reason for investor underperformance is that investors often end up exhibiting counterproductive behavior such as selling a mutual fund too early or holding on to a stock too long—in other words, they fall prey to common decision traps. Often you may buy or sell the *wrong* investment at the *wrong* time for the *wrong* reason. Investors do not stay invested long enough to take advantage of long-term investment returns, as the average equity mutual fund investor has a holding period of just over three years, according to Dalbar.[6] Carl Richards found that people do not

4   C. Richards, *The Behavior Gap: Simple Ways to Stop Doing Dumb Things with Money* (New York: Penguin, 2012).
5   Dalbar, "Quantitative Analysis of Investor Behavior" (Boston: Dalbar, 2016).
6   Ibid.

invest for the long term; they trade and trade often.[7] Over the past twenty years, average investor returns have lagged investment returns by 4% to almost 11% annually.[8] Understanding these numbers are problematic will hopefully serve as a reality check about human nature and our propensity to make poor decisions, all the while believing we are doing the right thing. One of your financial advisor's primary objectives should be to help you close the gap that exists between investment and investor returns, by helping you monitor and manage your own behavior. Dalbar provides clear evidence of how poorly individual investors performed as compared to the S&P 500 Index over time (based on twenty-year annualized rates of return). Simply leaving money sitting in an index without touching it would have led to superior long-term returns. Instead, investors were likely doing things such as selling at the low and buying at the high and had actual returns that were significantly less than the market returns over the same period of time.

After this chapter, it is my hope that you'll have gained a better understanding and awareness of the ways in which we sabotage ourselves in our own decision making. Simply being mindful of these traps will help us overcome their inherent risks. However, a Money Navigator well-versed in these common decision traps can provide additional security in ensuring you don't fall prey to one or more of these traps when making important decisions. In the next chapter we'll discuss some of the reasons investors continually make self-sabotaging errors.

---

7   Richards, *The Behavior Gap.*
8   Dalbar, "Quantitative Analysis."

Chapter Takeaways

Cusp of Retirement

When you are closing in on retirement, you have a tendency to fall prey to the Opinion Trap. You create anchor points because you may have evaluated a lot of investment data over a long period of time in order to arrive at an acceptable conclusion. The result is you drop anchor and neglect to make an adjustment even though the reason for the conclusion at which you arrived may no longer be relevant. This could mean that the investment you have chosen is now inappropriate for your situation and could wreak havoc on your FinLife® plan. To this point, when you are on the cusp of retirement, sequence of return risk is amplified. This means that markets ebb and flow, and when the tide ebbs (bear markets) it can ebb for a few years in a row. So, if the timing of your retirement is predicated on a certain level of investable assets, you need to allocate your portfolio in such a manner that drawdown risk is not unacceptably large due to ebbing markets. Being aware of the impact of anchoring and the Opinion Trap can help you to lessen the effects of these issues.

Already Retired

The common decision trap that I have seen impact those already in retirement over the years is the As-Is Trap. You think, "Why should I change anything? It's always worked fine the way I've done it in the past." This could be in relation to the clothes you buy, where you shop for food, go on vacation, or how you invest. The message for you in this chapter is by becoming more self-aware, you can minimize the impact of falling victim to your own behavioral biases, such as adhering to the status quo. This will result in a more open approach to new ideas that could improve the probability of success of your FinLife® plan.

Facing a Life Transition

Maybe you just graduated from college and now you have your first job. Right now, you are sitting there on *your* sofa in *your* apartment reading *your* book while eating *your* food. Truly exciting? Absolutely. Scary at the same time? Most definitely! Where the heck do you even begin to think about investing?

As a newly minted graduate, one of the first rules of finance you can learn is it's not *timing* the market, but rather *time in* the market that counts. This simply means that it is counterproductive to sell investments in a panic at the wrong time for the wrong reasons. Learning how to manage decision traps by understanding your emotions, rather than simply reacting to them, will help you to improve upon the gap that exists between investment returns and investor returns. Additionally, if you start investing early through your 401k with your first job, you are setting yourself up for long-term success financially.

Another easy rule of finance is the Rule of 72. It's pretty simple really: You take the number 72 and divide it by whatever rate of return you can earn on an investment, and the result is how many years it will take your money to double in value. So for example, if I could reasonably earn 6% per year on my money, I would double it in approximately twelve years. Pretty cool, huh? Well, what's really great is what happens when you get the fourth or fifth double, meaning you stay invested over a long period of time and see your money benefit from what Einstein called the Eighth Wonder of the World, compound interest!

CHAPTER 5

Not Enough Time and Too Many Decisions

*"The difference between school and life? In school, you're
taught a lesson and then given a test. In life, you're given a
test that teaches you a lesson."*
—Tom Bodett

L et's say you are in the process of trying to find information on
the best places to retire in the United States. How do you start?
I would venture to guess that you'd probably Google it. Then
Sergey Brin and Larry Page (Google's founders) would serve up
only 51,900,000 results—this number changes every day, of course, but try
it and you'll see! What the heck do you do with over fifty-one million
hits on your topic of interest? How do you make sense of it all? It could
literally take a lifetime to evaluate. You want to know the answer to your
personal question—the best place to retire for you! How can you possibly
build out any kind of decision matrix to help yourself make a choice?

Among other things, this book aims to equip you with the self-awareness to move forward toward your Ideal FinLife®. In the previous chapter,
we discussed in depth the possible pitfalls you may find yourself up against
when making investing decisions. This chapter discusses another possible
derailer to your goals: having too much information to know what to
do with it. While a Money Navigator—your personal CFP®—can help
you sift through that information, it is also my hope that this chapter will
help you understand that this is a universal problem that we all must work

through in order to make meaningful, informed decisions. As discussed earlier in the book, information is *not* education. Information has been commoditized to the point where much of it is just noise. It loses value because of its abundance, frequency, and accessibility. Don't misunderstand: Having more information is a great thing, but having too much information causes paralysis and lack of relevance to one's personal situation and unique set of circumstances. It causes us to lock up and not know what to do. The old saying "paralysis by analysis" is oh so true.

The one commodity that is significantly valued in today's culture and that we are all starved for is *time*: time to do what we need to do whether it's work, family, or leisure pursuits. Our time-deprived lives are only exacerbated by the information overload that requires decision making and choices to be made. Sometimes the choices are quite simple, and the results of the choices may be benign and not impactful long term, such as finding the best plumber today to fix the leak in the sink. However, other times the choices are significant, the stakes much higher, and the resultant actions can have ripple effects for years—think planning for retirement, for example.

If you agree with me that you are receiving an overload of information but lacking the time you need to do everything you need to do, then how can you know with confidence you are making the right decisions at the right time for your life? How can you process everything with certainty and confidence? Most people can't—they need someone to provide support. Unfortunately, when it comes to your financial life, there are not many "do-overs" when it comes to the choices you make. Stakes are high: You need to get it right the first time. You need someone who can look at the whole picture and make sense of it with you, and for you. This chapter aims to show you how a *Money Navigator* can help you sift through the information overload, and gives you some tips for understanding the best ways of achieving that goal.

Put Some Right-brain Thinking into It, Really... Elon Musk Is Doing It!

Daniel Pink's book *A Whole New Mind* was published in 2006, but I would argue that it is even more relevant today.[1] Pink's thesis is that right-brain thinking is every bit as important, if not more so, than left-brain thinking in today's society. The subtitle of the book is *Why Right-brainers Will Rule the Future*, and I believe the future is now. Right-brain thinking is the creative part of the brain utilized most by painters, sculptors, designers, and individuals who can conceptualize and contextualize lots of information. Left-brain thinking, in a general sense, is the logical side of the brain; think STEM (science, technology, engineering, and math). These are the folks who are the logicians—they could be accountants, architects, computer scientists, or engineers, for example. Left-brain folks can often run circles around most people with respect to their ability to do mathematical calculations, solve complex problems, analyze large amounts of data, and design structures or systems. While it may seem like you'd need to utilize left-brain thinking most to achieve results in your investments, the surprising conclusion I've reached is the opposite—the following story illustrates why.

I recently attended a conference at my daughter's all-girls high school in the Washington, DC, area. It was a fabulous session where graduates came back to the campus to hold a Q&A session with the current students. The topic of the conference was STEAM, which is the aforementioned STEM but with an "A" added in for the arts. The first graduate discussed how she was an aerospace engineer who had gone on to graduate with a master's in space policy and was now working for SpaceX, Elon Musk's company. A second graduate had earned two master's degrees in the UK, one in English literature and one in book preservation. She was now pursuing a third master's degree, this one in chemistry, in order to be a more qualified and effective book preservationist! The final presenter had been premed but then transitioned into mechanical engineering. She said she always had the desire to go into medicine, but she discovered she did not have the passion to become a doctor. Instead, although she still pursued a career in the medical field, she was now designing human joints, such as shoulders, hips, and knees. I was so impressed by these young women who had pursued careers in engineering and the arts and was thankful that my daughter was being exposed to these success stories.

---

1   D. H. Pink, *A Whole New Mind: Why Right-Brainers Will Rule the Future* (New York: Riverhead Books, 2005).

However, the most interesting part of the day for me came at the very end, during the Q&A. One of the high school students stood up and asked the aerospace engineer what type of educational background SpaceX was currently looking for in their new hires. The engineer said that she'd like to say SpaceX was hiring lots and lots of engineers—her passion, of course. To my surprise she said that not only was SpaceX not hiring an overabundance of engineers, they weren't even hiring many MBAs. Instead SpaceX was hiring MFAs, or masters of fine arts graduates—right-brainers! Yes, that's right, right-brainers. Think about it for a second: Elon Musk's car company, Tesla, has had tremendous success due to its engineering capabilities—that is for certain. But a big part of Tesla's success is its ability to incorporate cutting-edge design in their vehicles. Design requires creativity beyond being a logician, and MFAs provide exactly that for Tesla. SpaceX is simply following the successful formula that Tesla has already utilized. As we walked to the car after the session, I encouraged my daughter to continue to pursue the career in architectural engineering that she so loves, but to sprinkle more art classes into her curriculum. She has responded by not only taking the various math and science courses which are required for her to pursue architecture, but by taking drawing, ceramics, and sculpting classes as well.

Being able to think outside the box is a critical tool when it comes to handling information overload. Just like the MFA who will be hired by SpaceX for her creative bent, you must be able to creatively conceptualize and contextualize all of the information available and make it relevant to you. Your Money Navigator is equipped to do exactly this, and can provide you with guidance when you are faced with any decision that can impact you financially. As I mentioned earlier in the book, notice that I did not say "any *financial* decision that can impact you." There is a distinct difference that requires your financial advisor to be an artist of sorts—to be able to think outside the box, or to not even use the box at all!

Your Personal Decision Matrix

In the previous section, I outlined the importance of utilizing right-brain thinking. However, this is not to say using your left-brain thinking is not equally important! One of the most helpful tools you can use when it comes to handling information overload is a personal decision matrix.

When presented with an important choice, this tool can assist you in arriving at a satisfying conclusion. You can utilize the personal decision matrix both on your own and with the expertise and guidance of your Money Navigator, who can help you create a system that enhances your decision-making process.[2] A personal decision matrix is made up of four specific decision traps, one in each quadrant. The matrix is designed to help you through each of these four traps to make sure you're not falling victim to them when trying to make a choice. It's a process you should go through in order to arrive at better decision.

I'll walk you through the process of using a personal decision matrix by using an earlier example. Say you were using Google to search for

---

2   Chip and Dan Heath provide a great framework for implementing better choices in both life and work in their best-selling book *Decisive: How to Make Better Choices in Life and Work* (New York: Crown Business, 2013).

the top retirement spots in the US. In order to start to build out your personal decision matrix, you first need to familiarize yourself with the sort of information that's out there. You now have over fifty-one million choices to review. This assists you in looking at the choice you have encountered (in this case, the opportunity of moving to a great new city for your retirement) from the correct perspective and not falling victim to the Myopia Trap that we discussed earlier in the book. Remember, the Myopia Trap results in you narrowly framing the choice, which may cause you to overlook certain things or miss opportunities. By building out your personal decision matrix with an abundance of options, you will have ample information to begin to narrow your set of choices as you use three additional strategies in concert with casting a wide net.

The Confirming Evidence Trap is the next landmine you need to look out for when building out your personal decision matrix. Let's say your cousin moved to Naples, Florida, in retirement and she has been harping on you for years to join her in your retirement. During your search, you can automatically and unknowingly begin favoring Naples as the choice, even though you are trying to make an objective decision. As choices appear, you begin to gravitate toward Naples because the city "has everything that I've been looking for," but you prematurely dismiss other cities as viable options. You are an insider with respect to your own choice, so you need to step outside of yourself in order to see things through a different lens. This requires you to use reflective thinking and engage your brain a bit to craft questions you can ask yourself about the choice at hand. "Have I thought about how expensive it will be to find a home in Naples?" or "Am I only considering Naples because my cousin lives there?" or "Shouldn't I also consider Ft. Myers or perhaps even Vero Beach?" You want to make sure you are providing yourself with greater clarity and objectivity. An independent financial advisor who is a Money Navigator can assist in this endeavor because without help, the reality of what should be a fun exercise results in something quite stressful and a bit overwhelming.

The Disproportionate Pain Trap is the next component of the personal decision matrix. Similar to what we just discussed with the Confirming Evidence Trap, the Disproportionate Pain Trap requires you to look at the choices presented to you from an outside-in perspective. We are predisposed to be loss averse, and numerous studies have shown that the pain of losing is far greater than the pleasure of winning similar amounts.

Evaluating your choices from a different vantage point can be enlightening and empowering at the same time. This requires reflective or System II thinking, as Daniel Kahneman calls it in *Thinking, Fast and Slow*. System II requires you to use your logical brain as opposed to your intuitive brain when making a decision. It requires more energy but helps you to remove the fight-or-flight response. The fight-or-flight response goes back to the days when the caveman had to make intuitive decisions or die—think saber-toothed tiger! Most of the time, your decision matrix is not a hurry up and decide situation that results in do or die, so taking your time and not rushing to judgment is imperative.

The Overconfident Forecast Trap is the final component of the personal decision matrix. Once you have decided, you tend to project what the future will look like based upon the choices you have made. But what if your assumptions prove to be incorrect? If you are overconfident about your prospects going forward, any bump in the road can be jolting at the least and extremely disruptive at the worst. To avoid this trap, you have to have a Plan B in the event that your Plan A is wrong. This requires additional options to be added to your personal decision matrix. For example, if you move to Naples, but then five years into retirement you realize that your cash flow is not enabling you to live the lifestyle you expected, perhaps a move to a lower-cost area would be necessary.

Bottom line: using your left-brain thinking to create a decision matrix can help you build out a better framework for understanding how to make some of the biggest decisions in your life and allows you to process all the information at hand in the most meaningful, actionable way.

When it comes to handling information overload, both left- and right-brain thinking will come in handy. You can benefit from practicing creative right-brain thinking when it comes to finances. A Money Navigator is well versed in thinking outside the box, and can help push you in the right direction with his creative solutions. At the same time, left-brain thinking is also important and can help you gain a better understanding of all the options in front of you. In the next section of the book, I'll discuss the overabundance of financial products, financial advisors, and companies available today and how they are often misunderstood.

Chapter Takeaways

Cusp of Retirement

You are likely going to investigate topics related to your retirement at one time or another. As you enter the cusp years, your decisions are going to ramp up considerably because you feel a time crunch. The issue you will undoubtedly face is choice overload. There is far too much information out there for our consumption, and it is easy to fall into the trap of trying to digest it all at the same time. The Money Navigator can help you sift through your choices so you can derive a solid conclusion on the issue with which you are concerned. The example we discussed in this chapter about places to retire is a perfect illustration of this important point. We've seen that narrowing information down and having a system to consider what you have filtered is important.

Already Retired

When you first retired, logically it made sense to you to file for Social Security, but after you had a chance to discuss this with the Money Navigator you realized that if you looked at it from a right-brain perspective, perhaps you could find a new source of income. You're still passionate about what you do, you have a lot of fuel left in the tank, and companies will pay you for what you know or know how to do, so why not? It's easy to fall into the trap of following a logical, left-brain progression when evaluating a financial issue related to your retirement. It makes perfect sense to think retirement and file for Social Security, but when utilizing a new lens you can now see the merits of bringing some creativity into your FinLife® planning. Right-brain thinking, in this case, enables you to follow your passion to enjoy doing what you do best professionally, while at the same time deferring Social Security income so you will receive a greater benefit when you decide to file a few years later. Life is not all numbers. In fact, life is much more about people and their emotions, as we have and will continue to discuss throughout the book.

Facing a Life Transition

Life transitions are often not planned, and many times are not welcome. You may be reeling from a divorce, a death, or an unexpected move, but during this difficult time the Money Navigator can help you to consider other issues that require your immediate attention in order to move forward with your FinLife®. Based on confirming evidence you have received, you may think that you need to move to a new location or get involved with where your kids will be going to school.

As an example, you have gone through a divorce and you are experiencing a disproportionate amount of pain because all you can sense is the loss you have experienced. The Money Navigator can provide you with a right-brain-oriented, outside-in perspective on the situation because he or she is not enveloped by the raw emotions that are exposed at this time. Eventually, you may arrive at a conclusion regarding these two issues and others, but you tend to overconfidently project the results of these conclusions into the future. A remedy for this would be to use your left-brain thinking to evaluate additional options before making a final decision. These are issues that simply cannot be shelved, so the Money Navigator will not only bring them to the forefront, but also help you to effectively evaluate these situations and choices in a timely fashion. Someone who can provide the colander to help filter ideas that we talked about earlier is most necessary when emotions are running rampant and objective thinking can be difficult.

The Financial Services Industry Landscape

"Not everything that can be counted counts, and not everything that counts can be counted."

— *Bruce Cameron*, Informal Sociology: A Casual Introduction to Sociological Thinking

CHAPTER 6

Product Proliferation and Marketing

"Americanism: Using money you haven't earned to buy
things you don't need to impress people you don't like."
— *Robert Quillen*

There is an overabundance of investment choices for investors in the financial services marketplace today. Even as a financial advisor I see the dizzying array of options that I could offer to my clients. It's another example of choice overload. In the context of financial product overload, I combat this situation by working with business partners who act as information funnels or "human browsers" that use strict criteria and due diligence processes to enable me to narrow the product options so I view them in context for me and ultimately my clients' needs, objectives, and goals. It makes sense for you to have a similar structure in place for making heads or tails of the abundance of financial information or, more likely, to outsource the responsibility to someone else. This is why my firm belief is in hiring a qualified CFP® professional who will put you on the fast track to attaining this objective. This individual is your ***Money Navigator***. This section will give you a broad view of the financial services landscape, including everything from products to services offered, to utilizing a financial advisor versus a Money Navigator. In explaining this landscape, you'll have a better idea of why the Money Navigator is the best choice you can make in terms of seeking help in managing your FinLife®. We'll start in this chapter by looking into other products on the market. Let's dive in!

A Non-technical Explanation of the Primary Financial & Insurance Products

There are numerous categories of investments and insurance products. For the sake of brevity and simplicity, I've outlined the most common types of investments and insurance, and ones the average individual has access to in Appendix 2.

Vertical Integration: Manufacturers Are the Distributors

When I first got started in the financial services industry over twenty-five years ago, I worked for a large insurance company. The company was, and still remains, a major player in the industry and is multinational in focus. The firm had a sizeable salesforce and was considered a captive organization. A captive organization is a product manufacturer that also has a distribution system—in this case a salesforce. The company develops their own investment or insurance products, then sells them directly to the marketplace—hence the word "captive." Captive agents can only sell proprietary products, those designed by the company.

Over the years this distinction has become blurred somewhat as captive organizations have aligned themselves with brokerage outfits that provide product from outside/competing companies, but to be perfectly honest, a manufacturer that has distribution (i.e. fully vertically integrated) incents its salesforce to sell their own investments products first. Sometimes the incentives are not direct, in the form of dollars paid, but more perks such as exotic vacations and preferred treatment in the company.

The captive approach for obvious reasons relies on favoritism toward the parent company providing the products. I never felt comfortable working in this type of situation, so I started my own independent registered investment advisory firm over two decades ago. I wanted to be able to help my clients make smart decisions that could impact their lives financially, not push proprietary products that might not be suitable for them. I wanted a situation whereby I could use any product without pressured sales tactics from my employer. Under this format, my interests would be aligned with my clients and I would be paid for my financial advice and guidance. Doing the right thing for the client at the right time was paramount to me. I voted in favor of open architecture.

Open architecture is a way of describing the nonproprietary landscape provided by a product agnostic company. This means that financial advisors who are practicing their craft in this type of environment are operating as fiduciaries (more on this later in the chapter) for their clients. It means that the financial advisors can utilize any product they need to use in order to assist clients in attaining their goals. Since compensation is on a fee basis, the financial advisor is not incented to sell one product over another.

Should I Use a Bionic Advisor?—The Advent of the Robos

A robo-advisor is a type of financial advisor that provides portfolio management and some light financial planning online with minimal human intervention or interaction. Over the past couple of years, these types of companies have mushroomed, as we are in a seven-plus-year bull market that has made passive, low-cost indexing strategies appear extremely popular, particularly to the DIY crowd. These types of strategies rely minimally on human touch and are simple to implement, often using inexpensive ETFs. Robo-advisors use algorithms to determine client allocations after clients provide inputs into a web interface.

Robo-advisors are here to stay, but until machine learning improves to the point of a robo-advisor being able to evaluate your situation and tell you not to invest $20,000 with them because it is a bad financial move and instead pay down $20,000 in high-interest credit card debt because it is better for you, the robos are not actually providing advice. No, instead, the robo-advisors are order-takers, plain and simple, and I don't see this changing anytime soon. To be clear, I am not anti-robo, as I do think there is a place for the robo-advisor as a stand-alone solution or as a digital enhancement to the financial advisor's practice offerings. The latter solution enables the Money Navigator to become truly bionic—an empathetic and skilled human being who has all of the latest digital tools for your benefit!

RIAs, IARs, Wirehouse Brokers, Independent B/Ds, Registered Reps, the SEC, and FINRA—What's With All the Acronyms?

RIAs are Registered Investment Advisors who are regulated by the SEC (Securities and Exchange Commission) if they have over $100 million in assets under management, and those firms managing less than $100 million are regulated by the state. IARs (Investment Advisor Representatives) work for RIAs. Wirehouse brokerage firms are the traditional stock brokerage companies, such as Merrill Lynch, Morgan Stanley, UBS, and Wells Fargo. Registered Representatives are employees of wirehouses and independent B/D (Broker-Dealer) firms, and they are regulated by the FINRA (the Financial Industry Regulatory Authority).

The fastest growing segment of the aforementioned list is the independent advisory channel, the RIA. There are distinct reasons for this. Consumers have become disenfranchised with the wirehouse model, as investors become weary of their primarily pushing products and viewing their clients as walking wallets. The independent B/D channel is in maintenance mode at best, as this model is really a hybrid between the wirehouse and RIA model, and more sophisticated clients understand this fact. There are solid B/D firms out there, but the fact remains that the regulatory landscape in which they operate doesn't lend itself to the objectivity of the RIA space. Now let's clear the air about some confusing stuff.

The Fiduciary and Registered Representative Conundrum—Consumer Confusion Abounds

An Investment Advisor Representative (IAR) working for an RIA (Registered Investment Advisory firm) has a fiduciary responsibility to his clients. This means that, by law, he or she must put clients' interest first at all times. Similarly, CFP® professionals have a fiduciary responsibility to their clients. Registered representatives, on the other hand, have a bifurcated fiduciary responsibility to their firm *and* to their clients as a result of new Department of Labor (DOL) legislation. Under the new DOL regulations, registered representatives must serve clients in a fiduciary capacity when servicing ERISA plans such as 401ks. They also must serve in a fiduciary capacity when servicing IRA accounts as well. As of this writing, there is nothing in the DOL legislation regarding nonqualified (taxable) accounts, so the suitability standard still reigns for now—registered representatives have to ascertain suitability with respect to their client recommendations, and this is required to be documented and on file as part of the firm's "sales practices." Ascertaining suitability is a much lower standard than a fiduciary standard, whereby there could literally be dozens and dozens of suitable products for a client, but are they the best thing for the client from a fiduciary perspective? Unfortunately, many times they are not. This should matter to you a great deal because when you are receiving advice from a fiduciary, you should be confident that your advisor's interests are aligned with yours for *all* of your accounts, not just your 401k and IRA, and that there are no undisclosed conflicts of interest.

What about the robo-advisors? Can they be considered fiduciaries? I would think not, since they are not human and can't deliver individual advice, at least at this point. Additionally, robo-advisors don't go through a discovery process that helps human advisors understand their clients. How does a robo-advisor know that you have a special needs child, and about the resultant trust that was created for him, for example? You likely have many different financial needs but only a limited amount of money with which to fulfill those needs. Judgment and experience are required in order to act in a fiduciary capacity. Robo-advisors do not get to check either box in this regard.

Conflicts of interest can still exist in a fiduciary setting, but the critical thing here is that the conflicts must be fully disclosed to you. When working with a fiduciary, with proper disclosure, you needn't be concerned about hidden fees and sales incentives for your advisor to push certain products over others that are available. This is not the case when working with a registered representative and is usually apparent if you look at a monthly statement from a client at a wirehouse firm or B/D. The common theme is proprietary products strewn throughout the clients' account statements. So what type of firm should you consider? You should work with an independent RIA who operates under a fiduciary standard so you receive unbiased, objective, and bespoke advice for your unique set of circumstances. I advocate for the Money Navigator in this regard.

Compensation Methods

There are five fee models in the industry today. *Fee-only* is exactly what it sounds like. You pay the financial advisor a fee for helping you with your financial planning and investment management. This could be hourly, package, retainer, or based upon a percentage of your assets under her management. The second, *fee-based*, is a combination of fee-only coupled with earning commissions, usually on insurance product implementation. The third is a *retainer* arrangement, which could be part of a fee-only approach or coupled with a fee-based approach. The basic premise here is you pay your financial advisor a set amount each year (the retainer) and if any insurance products are used, a commission could also be paid. The fourth is a *commission* arrangement whereby your advisor charges commissions for buying and selling investments and insurance. The fifth is a *hybrid* approach, which is any combination of the aforementioned methods. Which type of arrangement is best for you? It's going to depend upon your personal preference, but I would argue that a fee-based approach is a notable method worth your consideration because it aligns the advisor's interest with yours without ignoring or de-emphasizing key planning areas, such as insurance, which are sometimes neglected, marginalized, or overemphasized under other methods.

At the end of the day, when you hire a financial advisor, you want to know that you are hiring someone for their intellectual property—this is the space between their ears that generates specific unbiased guidance, advice, and direction for you. This is what you pay your CPA, attorney, or doctor for, so why shouldn't it be the same way with your financial advisor? After all, this is complex stuff that we are dealing with here, so make sure you are hiring a pro who has your best interest at heart. The **Money Navigator** is exactly that person.

Chapter Takeaways

Cusp of Retirement

Let's say, as an example, you think you're three years away from retiring because you will be turning sixty-five, and that's the age you've always had in mind for retirement. Whether you can make this a reality or not is a question to which you really don't have an answer. A friend referred you to an excellent online service she used, so you decided to enter all of your financial data into a questionnaire and you answered some questions that the computer program asked you about your goals, objectives, and time frames. Seems simple enough. You're hoping that this interaction with a robo-advisor will provide you with clarity, confidence, and control about your FinLife®. It's easy and should be effective, right?

As part of your retirement planning, you would like to start a new business. You aren't sure if you should do this or not and you don't know if should put some financial projections together, much less a business plan. How should you organize, as an S Corp, C Corp, LLC? Do you need financing? How much personal capital will you need to contribute? How will this impact your FinLife® plan? Will you have employees? Do you need to lease space? What are the tax ramifications? Should you even be using sixty-five as your retirement age or is there a possibility you can put off taking Social Security, starting up your new business while still gainfully employed?

You get the point, as the list goes on and on. Conspicuously, there are no questions proffered by the robo-advisor about any of these issues that are obviously an important part of your financial planning. If you were instead working with a Money Navigator, that person could help you carve the path you desire toward your retirement.

Already Retired

In this scenario, let's say you've been working with John, a financial advisor with a large insurance company, for many years. John has always provided you with great advice, or so you thought. On the advice of a friend, you decide to meet with a Money Navigator. After visiting with the Money Navigator to receive a second opinion, you now realize that all of John's solutions over the years involved either products that his employer's company manufactures and/or on which he earned a commission. Initially this is upsetting to you, but the Money Navigator is quick to point out that John's recommendations appear to be suitable based upon your situation and given that his hands were tied to only offering his company's product suite. There are other products out there that may work better for your situation, based upon a fiduciary standard of care. You yearn for something different, someone different. You have decided that you want to work with someone who is sitting on the same side of the table as you, so you hire a Money Navigator to help guide you throughout the remainder of your retirement.

Facing a Life Transition

Let's say a headhunter has informed you that the job you have always wanted has become available at a competitor's company and you are on a short list for the position. You have always wanted to be the executive vice president of brand management. Adding to the mix is a generous salary and a robust executive benefits package including restricted stock units, bonuses, and deferred compensation. Logically you have to give the position some serious consideration, it would seem. "Yes, but..." you say. The "but" is you should not only use logical (left-brain) thinking to evaluate the position; you should also bring your creative right-brain into the mix. Let's think about how right-brain thinking could help bring clarity to this potentially life-changing experience. What kind of hours will you have to work? How much travel is involved? Can you work remotely if you desire? How much vacation time is permitted? Is continuing education paid for? How much autonomy will you have in the new position? Get the idea? This is not simply a quantitative exercise, as the qualitative aspects are, in many cases, more important. Having someone to talk through the different issues, and their impact on you financially and otherwise, could be the key to making the right decision for you. A Money Navigator can help even with a life-changing decision such as this one.

CHAPTER 7

Tools and Methods for Money–Value Alignment

"If you want to make changes in your future, you must make new choices today."
— Brian Tracy

As you know from the previous sections, if you are concerned about retirement planning, you should strongly consider the impact of behavioral finance and common investor decision traps on your overall financial picture. As human beings, we have the propensity to exhibit the biases discussed in this book that can be detrimental to your wealth. Implementing a well-diversified, tactically allocated portfolio can be an ideal way for you to offset the negative effects of poor decision making. This is what we will be diving into in-depth in this chapter.

It is imperative to note that financial decisions you make or do not make based upon your biases can be far more financially impactful, positively or negatively, than the rates of return earned on your respective investments. The following tools should not be viewed as the panacea or antidote to poor decision making; rather they are but a risk mitigation tool that should be considered as part of an overall plan. An experienced Money Navigator, versed in behavioral finance, investor decision traps, and Fixed Index Annuities (FIAs), can be an invaluable resource for you if you are approaching retirement or if you have already retired.

Four Primary Investment Strategies and Methodologies

There are four primary investment strategies that I utilize with my clients to help them toward living their ideal FinLife®. My firm utilizes an "Investor Preference Selection Dial" that enables me to use various degrees of the following: *performance, protection, low-cost tracking,* and *tax minimization.* I will review each one of these strategies so you can gain a better understanding of the pros and cons.

When implementing a *performance* portfolio, you are seeking higher returns in the long run. It is important to mention the time element in this context because during shorter periods of time you will find that volatility may be greater and therefore your principal may be subjected to increased drawdown risk (the risk of your account dropping significantly in value over a relatively short period of time due to a market decline). Because the strategies within a performance mandate are designed to seek alpha, or excess investment return over the relative benchmark, more trading may occur, which hinders the tax efficiency of a nonqualified (non IRA, non–tax deferred) account. Additionally, performance strategies are sometimes less likely to have inherent bear market protection because they can be considered more aggressive and less defensive strategies due to their alpha-seeking mandates. Alternative investments are included as part of performance portfolios. These could be investments that are not correlated to the stock and bond markets, which, as a result, provide greater diversification. Finally, patience is a virtue with performance types of strategies because it often takes a full market cycle or even longer to see the strategies pay off for the investor.

A *protection* portfolio is built upon the foundation of a strong defense being a great offense, so to speak. The primary goal of protection portfolios is to mitigate against the severest market declines. The idea is to utilize a tactical framework to evaluate quantitative and qualitative signals regarding the market and overall economy. These portfolios have the ability to be quickly reactive to various economic, market momentum, and financial stress/interest rate trends. These models cannot predict the market whatsoever, and if anyone ever tells you that is what their model does, run away as fast as you can because this simply runs counterfactual to most studies done on market timing. You cannot time the market! The reason you utilize tactical or protection portfolios is to minimize losses on the downside and get some return on the upside. What I've realized over the years is you want absolute returns in down markets (meaning 0% or greater) and participative returns in up markets (meaning you get at least 60–80% of the return). Like anything else in life, there are trade-offs with protection portfolios. Number one, protection portfolios are less tax-efficient due to the necessary trading that occurs due to repositioning assets on a daily, weekly, monthly, or quarterly basis. By utilizing an IRA for your protection allocations you can remove this negative. Another trade-off is historically you have less outperformance due to the protectionist bent of the portfolio. Finally, there are higher costs with these strategies due to the increased trading that may occur as a result of the positional output decisions that are by-products of the quantitative and qualitative signal evaluation.

An additional protection strategy I employ with clients is fixed index annuities (FIAs), which I will discuss in depth below. These are insurance contracts, not securities, and they provide optionality, or upside potential with no downside losses. FIAs provide an element of principal protection coupled with market participation. This strategy affords you the ability to earn a rate of return pegged to a market index (S&P 500 Index, Nasdaq 100, EuroStoxx 50, Barclays US Dynamic Balance Index, etc.) while having your principal guaranteed. For the downside guarantee, you end up giving up something on the upside, and that usually manifests itself in the form of cap or participation rates. For example, you may have the ability to earn up to 2% of the S&P 500 Index return each month or get up to a 6% annual cap on the Russell 2000 Index. These strategies are not meant to beat the market over the long term, but when they are included as part of an overall diversified asset allocation plan, they have been proven to be invaluable, especially during significant bear market declines. In fact, as I mentioned earlier, I wrote my doctoral dissertation on this very topic. If you want to learn more detail, then order my book on Amazon today. It's titled *Financial Economics of Index Annuities: An Analysis of Investor Returns*.

Low-cost tracking aims to have the lowest "hurdle rate" for your portfolio of investments. The hurdle rate is the rate your portfolio must earn to pay the internal expenses of the investment vehicles (mutual funds, exchange traded funds, etc.) in the portfolio plus whatever fee the financial advisor charges. In other words, you don't make any money until your hurdle rate is exceeded. Another goal of the low-cost tracking portfolio strategy is to track popular market indices, such as the S&P 500 Index or Barclay's Aggregate Bond Index, for example. By definition, there is no market outperformance with this strategy because you are essentially buying the market and its resultant performance. There is less bear market protection than a protection strategy because your investment portfolio returns are susceptible to however the markets perform. Additionally, there is less tax efficiency than a tax minimization strategy due to the passive approach to investment management.

A *tax minimization* strategy aims to lower portfolio taxes in the long run. Generally speaking there isn't usually any pretax outperformance with these strategies, but post-tax outperformance is possible due to tax-loss harvesting techniques, for example. This comes into play when you can sell losing investments and match the losses up with gains that have been harvested to minimize or negate taxation. There isn't any bear market protection with tax minimization strategies, and generally these strategies will be higher cost than some low-cost tracking and outperformance strategies.

The job of your financial advisor is to recommend an allocation that aligns with your overall risk profile, time frame, goals, and objectives. By using varying degrees of the aforementioned strategies, you can ensure that you have a world-class investment portfolio that can weather any storm. Appropriate investment allocations are essential to a solid FinLife® management plan.

Another Tool for Consideration: Fixed Index Annuities

Fixed Index Annuities (FIAs) are an increasingly popular but often misunderstood retirement planning vehicle. FIAs are insurance contracts designed as safe, secure, long-term, tax-deferred accumulation vehicles for retirement. The contracts are not intended to outperform the stock market, but instead have some upside participation in the returns of an external index such as the S&P 500 (you don't actually invest in the S&P, but your returns are "pegged" to its performance). FIAs are guaranteed against losses! Your account is guaranteed to never go down and regardless of what the market does, you will not lose any money.

But there has to be a trade-off, right? Yes: in life there is no free lunch. Since you receive complete downside protection, there is a cap on how much you can earn on the upside. Here are two examples of how this works.

1. If you have an *annual cap structure*, for example, your earnings in the S&P 500 Index may be limited to, say, 5.5% per year. So if the S&P goes up by 6%, you receive 5.5%. If the S&P goes up by 12%, you receive 5.5%. Finally, if the Index goes down by 20%, you receive a 0% return.

2. If you have a *monthly cap structure*, you could earn up to 2% per month in the contract. Let's say in the first month the S&P went up by 3%, well, you'd earn 2%. If in month two, the S&P went down 2%, you would register a -2% rate of return. At the end of twelve months all twelve of your monthly returns are added together, positives and negatives, and the result is what you earn. So let's say the total was 8%. Then your contract would grow by 8% and you would establish a new high-water mark that your contract could not go below. Conversely, if the total of all twelve months was -8%, your return would be 0% and you would not have lost any money. *Complete downside protection with upside opportunity!*

These intrinsic qualities make FIAs a vehicle worthy of consideration for you in order to counteract the harmful impact of the common investor decision traps discussed in chapter 4.

FIAs may help you to neutralize many of your natural human tendencies that lead to poor *investor* returns (remember the difference between this term and "investment returns," also discussed in chapter 4). As a reminder, investor return is how your portfolio performed over a specific period of time, with your biases and actions taken into account. Investment return is the return earned by an actual investment vehicle over a particular period of time. As we previously discussed, historically, average investor returns are significantly less than investment returns.

FIAs are not new to the marketplace, having been around since the mid-1990s when Keyport Life developed the first contract. Over the past five to ten years FIAs have become popular tax-deferred savings vehicles, as evidenced by the fact that sales of FIAs have produced hockey stick–like growth charts. In addition to the aforementioned characteristics, many FIAs also have income features embedded within the contracts. Similar to fixed annuities, you have the option of annuitizing an FIA so you receive a guaranteed stream for a set period of years or for the rest of your life. The positive is you receive a guaranteed income, but the negative if you annuitize is that you have forgone your principal (although some contracts have residual refund options). This may make sense for you, but if not and you still require income, there is another option available with FIAs: income riders.

Income riders provide you with withdrawal guarantees (where you don't have to annuitize the contract, and therefore you do not give up access to your principal) that provide you with a steady, potentially ever-increasing stream of income payments that can be turned on or off depending upon your needs and circumstances. This means that *you haven't given up access to your money.* These payments never decrease and can be continually increasing because the FIAs continue to participate in market returns, which in turn can impact your monthly income positively.

FIAs: What's the Catch?

How can the insurance companies provide these guarantees? You might be thinking, "It seems too good to be true that you can get part of the upside, but none of the downside." This is an important question, so let's discuss how this is done.

When you purchase an FIA, about 90% of the funds are invested in long-term bonds that pay a steady rate of interest. This is how the insurance company can offer you the downside guarantees and principal protection because *this money is never invested in the stock market.* The remaining 10% is split between buying options contracts (mostly call options) on the index that is being utilized, such as the S&P 500 or Russell 2000, for example, and agent compensation. To be clear, when you buy an FIA you are never invested in the stock market at all. Instead, *you have purchased a contract from the insurance company* that is a temporal obligation—essentially, this means that the insurance company has agreed to certain things over time and you have agreed that you won't pull your money out for a specific period of time. The return you can earn is pegged to a stock market index, which simply means you will receive interest credits if the index goes up, but as we have mentioned previously, you will not participate in the market index if it goes down. The insurance company has hedged its portfolio and its obligations to you by holding the options contracts. You *do not* own the options; you own an insurance contract. If the market goes up, you will receive gains, which are locked in (more on this next), and if the market goes down, the options will expire unexercised, and there will be no losses in your account.

Let's say you bought an FIA for $200,000 and you earned 5.5%. Your account would be credited with $11,000 in interest and your new floor value would be $211,000 going forward. Again, your gains are locked in each and every year. This is an extremely important concept with respect to the benefit of FIAs as part of an overall portfolio. Think about what happened in 2008 and 2009. The markets collectively dropped over 50% during that time frame. Had you invested in an FIA, you would have lost absolutely nothing! Then when the market recovered (and it always recovers, by the way, even if you thought the sky was truly falling), you would begin to participate in the recovery from your floor value. I know, pretty incredible, right?

You may be thinking, "That's great, Paul, but how are participation and cap rates determined?" On the surface, it seems like the insurance company can just offer whatever cap rates they feel like offering. To an extent this is true, since an FIA is an insurance contract and *not* a security, but if an insurance company, say ABC Co., decided they were going to offer lower or higher cap rates than other FIA products on the market, they would need to be prepared for at least two eventualities. The first eventuality—what if ABC offered lower cap rates than the current FIA market? Keeping all things constant, this should result in a decrease in new business for ABC. This makes intuitive sense because if competitors' cap rates are higher, they would provide you, the investor, with the ability to make more money by using their FIA over FIAs issued by ABC. The second eventuality—conversely, if ABC made their cap rates higher than their competitors', they would see an influx of new business (at least for a little while) because you would know that you had the opportunity to make more money by buying ABC's FIAs over the others available on the market. Under this scenario ABC could end up having such a large inflow of business that their service levels would drop considerably because they are not staffed appropriately to process the significant amount of new business applications that they receive.

I had the pleasure of hearing John Olsen, a financial advisor and author, speak at my local Financial Planning Association symposium meeting a few years ago. He gave a wonderful presentation about FIAs and explained the relationship between interest rates and options prices with participation and cap rates. Take a look at the scenario outlined below and you'll be able to follow this quite easily.

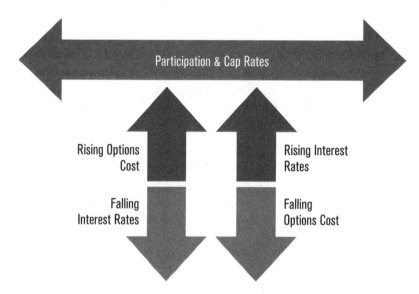

Chart constructed as a result of hearing John Olsen's speech: "Fixed Index Annuities." Speech presented at Financial Planning Association Winter Symposium in Dulles Hyatt, Dulles, Virginia, January 2011.

As interest rates go down, cap rates go down because the insurance company earns less on its bond portfolio (remember, about 90% of the FIA money is invested in long-term bonds). Generally speaking, as interest rates rise, the insurance company can increase their spread (earnings that they make) so they can afford to offer more attractive caps and participation rates. All companies are swimming in the same pond, so to speak, so you tend to see caps and participation rates converge around a mean (kind of like a bell-curve distribution). Separately, as the stock market becomes more volatile (this is usually measured by the VIX, which is an indicator of how volatile the market is), then options prices increase. This is the case because with increased volatility comes increased uncertainty.

This phenomenon causes options prices to escalate to compensate for the uncertainty. When options prices increase, the insurance company's costs of hedging the FIA increase, so caps and participation rates are lowered. There are only 100 cents in a dollar, so if the insurance company is spending more to provide the contractual guarantees, something has to give in order for them to make a profit. Conversely, when the volatility in the markets goes down, options prices decrease, which in turn provides the insurance company with the ability to offer higher caps and participation rates.

What about fees in the FIA? "I've always heard that annuities are bad because of the high fees." Unlike a variable annuity, when you purchase an FIA you will pay no internal management fees for the base contract. The only time there will be any fees assessed against your account is if you decide to elect an income rider, which I discussed earlier in this section. The income rider charges range anywhere from .50% to 1.25% annually, depending upon the benefit and insurance company offering the FIA. I often say that the primary fee in an FIA is *time*. You need to hold onto the FIA for the amount of time that you agreed to up front, whether it is five, seven, or ten years (the most common surrender periods). This is why it is so important to allocate a percentage of your overall portfolio that you are comfortable not having access to for a while in order to maximize the value of the FIA.

If you need to access your principal during the surrender period, you may do so, as most FIAs permit free 10% withdrawals annually. If you make this withdrawal prior to reaching age 59 ½, you will be assessed an additional 10% penalty by the IRS, because the IRS views FIAs as long-term retirement savings vehicles. Additionally, if you need to take out more than 10% in any given year, it is likely that you would pay a surrender penalty. Due to the reality of long-term care impacting so many individuals in this country, many FIAs permit you to withdraw up to the full account value penalty-free to cover nursing home care expenses.

Let's say you die prematurely. If you haven't started taking guaranteed income by annuitizing your principal, your FIA balance goes to your designated beneficiary(s). By annuitizing, you forego your principal, so unless you selected a refund option, there wouldn't be a death benefit payable to your heirs. That's why I like using the income rider approach to generating income in your FIA that we discussed earlier. Under that scenario, if you had already started taking guaranteed income (via the income rider, not by annuitizing), then your beneficiary(s) would receive the remaining balance left in your account after factoring in the withdrawals you made plus interest earned.

I'm often asked if you should put an IRA (Individual Retirement Account) into an FIA. You certainly should not do this if the sole objective is tax deferral. Why? Well, an IRA is already tax-deferred, so you do not need to wear a belt *and* suspenders. I suggest that you consider using an FIA for your IRA only if there were other benefits in the FIA that you could not get anywhere else. And as we have discussed, there are many benefits of utilizing an FIA in addition to tax deferral. The primary benefit is the ability to lock in gains and have complete downside protection for your IRA dollars.

The overarching theme here is *by utilizing FIAs you can avoid large market sell-offs and not concern yourself with the time it would take to recover big losses in your account.* When these types of declines have occurred in the past, the time it takes to recover from losses has ranged from two years to two decades! If you are on the cusp of retirement or already retired, there is no way you can handle having to deal with recovery periods like these.

How FIAs May Help You Avoid Decision Traps

I have spent years researching the ways in which FIAs can help to minimize the impact of the decision traps outlined in chapter 4, or even avoid them altogether. I've outlined the hows and whys of this below.

The Opinion Trap
The only volatility you will experience in an FIA will be positive.[1] Due to the downside protection afforded by FIAs, you are

1   FINRA, "Equity-Indexed Annuities—A Complex Choice," http://www.finra.org/investors/alerts/equity-indexed-annuities_a-complex-choice.

insulated from the effects of anchoring and resultant drawdown risk. This keeps the range of returns at 0% or greater, rather than subjecting the investment to a virtually limitless downside that exists in other vehicles.

The Internal Conflict Trap

FIAs can help you achieve consonance, which is the opposite of dissonance. Consonance is the simultaneous agreement or compatibility between two ideas, actions, or opinions. Two ways FIAs can help you combat cognitive dissonance are by preventing you from holding losing securities too long and throwing good money after bad. Perhaps you simply cannot convince yourself to sell a stock that you have purchased if you would realize a loss because this forces you to admit that your initial decision to purchase the stock was wrong. With FIAs, you won't experience market loss, which helps you to avoid this problem. Also, you may have invested in a losing stock and will continue to do so because of the sunk cost fallacy and selective attention. You figure you need to keep investing in the stock, because if you don't, you will have to admit you were wrong. You also tend to pay too much attention to the stock and ignore other factors that could potentially be helpful. FIAs help to avoid these issues since your principal is guaranteed, and if you are investing regularly, you won't be constantly buying in at a lower price. You also can be myopic in focus toward your FIA and not have to worry about other factors since it is protected from the market.

The Prudence Trap

FIAs can negate the need to process new information or complex data. The reason this is the case is because you do not need to concern yourself with negative information about a particular stock or even the S&P 500 Index. Normally, reading a negative quarterly earnings report on a stock you own or watching a talking head on TV pitching gloom and doom about the markets may cause stress and anxiety because, in both of these cases, your investments would likely go down in value as a result. When you own an FIA, you are protected from a market decline, and thus, you do not need to evaluate or process the new information. If you do evaluate the new information but do it at a suboptimal pace, it ultimately will not matter either, as FIAs are long-term contracts and don't require day-to-day management or timely decision making.

The Confirming Evidence Trap

FIAs can render irrelevant the fact that you may be in the dark regarding an investment because you have disregarded new, relevant information. If you have instead purchased a mutual fund and have not sought out any new information that could render your opinion negative on the fund, when an event occurs that negatively impacts your fund, you could be completely blindsided. Also, if you hold a substantial amount of your investable net worth in one stock, you are clearly underdiversified and your personal balance sheet could be decimated in short order. FIAs prevent these things from happening.

The Loss Recognition Trap

Simply put, by utilizing an FIA, you have removed the disposition effect or the unwillingness to recognize losses, because as we have previously reviewed, FIAs are guaranteed against losses so the point is moot.

The Rearview Mirror Trap

FIAs prevent your tendencies to view or describe history through your own biased lenses. Traditionally this occurs if you have a bad experience with an investment and you want to downplay its negative impact on your portfolio or your psyche. You are often deceiving yourself because you don't want to relive the pain or humiliation you felt for having made a poor decision. The FIA removes the need to use hindsight bias that occurs due to having chosen an investment that has lost money.

The Gambler's Trap

To be a successful investor it is imperative that you realize that it is an extremely difficult task to understand and follow such a dynamic, open-end, complex adaptive system as the stock market. Making it even more difficult is the fact that the markets are international in scope. If you use an FIA, you relieve yourself from the tasks of studying and tracking the markets. You can feel as if you are in control, and it is not an illusion!

The Disproportionate Pain Trap

Nullifying the possibility of any losses removes the concept of loss aversion from the investor equation. Since FIAs have guaranteed minimum values (initial premium plus locked-in gains minus any withdrawals), you know that your loss aversion bias will be kept at bay for this portion of your portfolio. Due to the phenomenon of loss aversion, what you really want are *absolute* returns in down markets and *participative* returns in up markets. FIAs deliver on these two parameters.

The Expert Trap

No matter how bad the market forecast (or it actually is), FIAs will protect you from a downturn. FIAs are protected from losses and you will not need to respond in a self-sabotaging fashion to any media's sensationalized storylines.

The Silo Trap

FIAs create a smoothing effect with respect to your portfolio returns in the aggregate over the long term. This can provide peace of mind and lessen the need to mentally monitor each account because an adequate amount is allocated in a foundational asset, the FIA. Your safe money (FIAs) buys your risk money (mutual funds, stocks, bonds, etc.) time; in this case, time for the portfolio as a whole to recover from possible negative volatility from riskier assets.

The Myopia Trap

Simply put, FIAs remove the risk of narrow framing bias, since market volatility does not negatively impact the value of the FIA.

The Overconfident Forecast Trap

With an FIA, you don't need to be concerned with having an overconfident forecast or underestimating downside risk. The reason is, every year you are given the parameters up front, as you will be provided with a range of returns, all positive, that are a possibility for you to earn, as the insurance company will declare the crediting rates on each policy anniversary date. For example, if you own an FIA with a 6% annual cap on the Standard & Poor's 500 Index, then you know that the most you can earn is 6% for the year, regardless of what the market is forecasted to do or how it actually performs.

The Probability Trap

This one is a bit counterintuitive. By exhibiting the representativeness bias, you align perfectly with the use of an FIA. When exhibiting representativeness, you adhere to your preconceptions by falling subject to base rate neglect, or the illusion of validity. If you own an FIA, adhering to the idea of owning the FIA ends up helping you remain invested in the contract (adhering to your original idea), avoiding neglecting base rates and not making the big mistake of selling at the wrong time.

The Self-Sabotage Trap

Since FIAs are long-term contracts, there is embedded forced self-discipline. In other words, the inherent lack of liquidity, similar to longer-term certificates of deposit, in an FIA may discourage undisciplined activity from occurring, albeit without a substantial penalty.

The "As Is" Trap

Initially this may not seem obvious in that FIAs are a great vehicle for someone who exhibits status quo bias because of the long-term contractual nature of FIAs. Paradoxically, since FIAs don't directly prevent status quo bias from occurring, it is okay for someone who is invested in an FIA to exhibit status quo bias because not doing so (surrendering the contract early) would cause the FIA owner to have to pay a penalty.

How Insurance Fits In and Why It Should Not Be Neglected

Insurance is a foundational tool in financial planning. Close your eyes and visualize a picture of the great pyramids in Egypt. The pyramids clearly had strong foundations. Similarly, you need insurance first, which is quite simply risk management and risk transfer. By purchasing an insurance contract, regardless of the type, you are deciding to transfer a risk you currently bear to a third party, the insurance company. If your current financial advisor is not addressing your overall insurance portfolio and planning with the same vigor and acumen as your investment management, that is a serious problem. By neglecting to analyze your insurance needs, you open yourself up to a whole host of risk management issues that could be detrimental to your financial well-being.

Think about it: what is your greatest asset? What asset could you simply not do without? The answer is your ability to earn a living! How do you insure that? Simple: you have adequate disability insurance so in case you become disabled and can no longer work, you'll still have income coming in to cover all of the bills that won't stop coming in just because you are not employed.

What if you're driving along on the highway and you accidentally rear-end someone? You both pull over to the side of the road and they see that you are driving a fairly nice automobile and you are dressed professionally. Then, all of a sudden, their neck just happens to start hurting. Three weeks later you have a lawsuit filed against you for $1 million. What just happened? In today's litigious society, this situation could occur any day, so why not have a personal umbrella liability policy of an adequate amount to cover these sorts of possibilities as opposed to not even thinking about it during your planning, only to be surprised if it took place?

If you died tomorrow, can you honestly say you know for certain that you own enough life insurance to enable your family to continue to live the lifestyle to which they have become accustomed? If you think you have the proper amount of insurance, do you know if you are paying too much? Do you own the appropriate type of life insurance based upon your goals, objectives, risk profile, and time frames? Do you still even need life insurance given your current stage of life? Does your spouse need life insurance or should you own policies on your children? Should you even personally own your life insurance or do you need a trust? Answering these and other questions is important in understanding that you need some sort of coverage, and in establishing how much is right for you.

Paying for long-term care expenses is another issue many individuals are facing today. This is due to the fact that we are all living longer, but eventually time catches up to us, and in many instances a long-term care illness is the result. These are expenses associated with home health care, assisted living, or nursing home care. Unfortunately, the cost of long-term care is not covered by Medicare or private health insurance, so the burden ends up falling upon you to cover this cost. Medicaid eventually will step in on a state-by-state basis, but this only occurs after you have spent down your assets to bare minimum levels. A prudent consideration is to have a long-term care insurance policy that will pay for these types of expenses so your estate isn't decimated. Most LTC policies can be purchased as young as age forty, but the majority of individuals buy the insurance in their fifties and sixties. The earlier you buy the insurance, the longer you will pay the premiums, but in aggregate the earlier you start, the less you'll pay over your lifetime. I often categorize LTC insurance as estate planning insurance while you are still alive. My point is, you could have the best estate plan out there for what should be done after you're gone, but if your estate is hit with tremendous out-of-pocket LTC costs, your estate plan doesn't mean much. You owe it to yourself to take a close look at LTC insurance by comparing several insurance policies for their benefits and costs as well as assessing your ability to self-insure against this potential expense.

When you build a house, the best foundations are not built upon sand. Similarly, when you build your financial and investment plans, the best plans are built upon strong risk management foundations. The great pyramids, which were built over 4,500 years ago, had strong and wide bases to enable them to tower above all of the previous man-made structures. Protect what you have first and then you can build out the rest of the plan from there. Doing it in reverse flips the pyramid upside down and makes no sense whatsoever.

How do you make sure that you are not exposed to these types of financially devastating occurrences? The solution is to hire a Money Navigator who is skilled in not only investment management but comprehensive FinLife® management, which by default includes insurance review, analysis, recommendations, and continual oversight.

From performance portfolios to insurance, the tools available to you are many when it comes to building out your FinLife® plan. Give yourself the best chance to be successful by investing in someone who knows the ins, outs, ups, and downs of each of these tools, and how they can specifically benefit your life and the life you want to lead in the coming years.

Chapter Takeaways

Cusp of Retirement

As you approach the next phase of your life, which in this case is your retirement, you'll need to figure out which financial tools you'll require to effectively accomplish the goal of retiring. One of the goals of this chapter was to provide you with a short list of investment and insurance ideas you may want to utilize leading up to your retirement. Many of the concepts can be carried over and utilized during your retirement years, which can make the transition from working to retirement a bit smoother.

For example, utilizing an FIA during the time leading up to retirement can help you to avoid the risk of large drawdowns on your capital at the expense of bad timing. As we discussed, FIAs are guaranteed against losses, so although you have the ability to earn returns based upon a market index, your principal is protected against market declines. This is a critical issue, particularly when you cannot afford to have large losses so close to the finish line of retirement.

Already Retired

Your asset allocation in retirement is an integral part of your FinLife® plan. Depending upon your income sources such as pensions, Social Security, and other income such as rental and other passive activities, your investments should be allocated in such a way that they generate additional income if it is needed. Additionally, you may want to have an element of growth in your portfolio as well, which lends itself to different strategies than those used just to generate income.

By zeroing in on the four primary investment strategies outlined in this chapter—performance, protection, low-cost tracking, and tax minimization—you can derive a portfolio allocation that is commensurate with your goals, objectives, income needs, and time frames. As a retiree, you may consider retreating from the market because you think since you are not earning a salary anymore you need to make sure that your principal stays intact. So what happens? You end up investing in bonds and CDs, for example. Being anxious about overexposure to the market during retirement is a valid concern, but due to increased life expectancies where you could live twenty, twenty-five, or even forty years in retirement, there likely needs to be an element of growth in your allocation. The Money Navigator can create a bespoke portfolio for you that takes this into account.

Facing a Life Transition

Earth-shattering is often what I hear when a client describes the emotion they experience when their spouse dies. Sometimes a longer-term illness was the culprit, which changes the dynamic of the relationship leading up to the death because frequently one spouse may be the primary caregiver. Other times, the death is more immediate and could have been a result of an accident or perhaps a sudden health event, such as a heart attack or stroke. Regardless of how the death occurred, the common denominator in these situations is the massive chasm of loss that manifests itself for the surviving spouse (and other family members).

As we discussed in this chapter, insurance planning is the foundational bedrock of sound FinLife® planning. In the scenarios described above, let's take a look at how insurance could have improved upon the overall picture. First off, disability insurance could have been utilized to replace income for the spouse, if still working, who got sick and was out of work for a few years battling cancer, for example. Second, if the ill spouse was retired, long-term care insurance could have been part of the equation in order to pay for the costs of home care for three years, which could easily approach and exceed $100,000 per annum. Finally, a life insurance plan could have been implemented in order to provide liquidity upon the death of the spouse, which would enable the surviving spouse to pay off debts as well as be invested to generate necessary cash flow. Having the insurance in place provides you with confidence that you are well-prepared to face any of the aforementioned unfortunate events.

CHAPTER 8

Not Just Another Financial Advisor

"Education is the most powerful weapon which you can use to change the world."
—Nelson Mandela

I n the previous chapter, I outlined the tools you have available to find success in your FinLife®—but as you have already gleaned from reading up until this point, the most important tool you can utilize is the professional advice of someone who works with individuals' finances for a living. Financial advisors are critical components of a successful retirement plan, but while all Money Navigators are financial advisors, not all financial advisors have the expertise and knowledge of the Money Navigator. In other words, these professionals don't carry the same depth of knowledge. So why should you seek out one rather than the other? The reasons are many—by the end of this chapter, you'll see what I'm talking about.

Perhaps a good way to describe the differences between the Money Navigator and a typical financial advisor is by telling you a brief story. Let's say there is a couple who have gone on a hike and they unfortunately find themselves lost in the woods. This could serve as a metaphor for a couple who are quickly approaching retirement and are perplexed with respect to what direction they should take to get to their destination of financial independence. While in the woods, the couple run into a financial advisor, and they tell the financial advisor their plight: They are lost and don't know what direction to take. The financial advisor points them in the right direction and sends them on their way. Inevitably, the couple end up back where they were, as they are lost again after going in a big circle. The couple still have a problem; they are still lost in the woods, as they don't know how to become financially independent. When they spot the financial advisor again, he gives them a compass and a map and sends them on their way. After a bit of time, once again, the couple end up back at the same spot because they either didn't know how to use the compass, or the map didn't exactly provide them with the best directions, as they may not have even been sure of where their starting point happened to be. So the couple are once again lost, confused, and looking for help. They haven't received clarity on how to retire on their terms.

If the Money Navigator sees the couple lost in the woods, he approaches the issue in a completely different fashion as a result of his mindfulness, hope, and compassion: empathy in action. What does the Money Navigator do? He doesn't simply tell the couple where to go and he doesn't only give them tools to use on their own. He tells the couple to hold his hand and he will personally lead them out of the woods to their destination. The couple can be confident in their ability to retire because the Money Navigator has helped them to focus on the things they can control in order to retire on their terms.

Perhaps one of the reasons you have tried the DIY approach to financial planning instead of hiring a professional was that you don't want to work with a salesperson, you don't have faith in the profession, or maybe you don't even think financial planning is a profession at all. You wouldn't be alone, and a big part of this problem is that the term "financial advisor" is riddled with public confusion and misperception. Additionally, it is far too easy today to become a financial advisor. Although there are some licensing requirements, the barriers to entry are relatively limited, and this needs to change, and it needs to change sooner rather than later.

Financial advisor has been synonymous with stockbroker, which to many individuals connotes financial salesperson. Most movies and television shows have portrayed stockbrokers as cutthroat salespeople, not trusted financial advisors. Also, think about the last time you were in a department store and the salesperson asked if you needed any assistance. What were the first words out of your mouth? "I'm just looking" and then you thought, "Just leave me alone" or "I don't want any sales pressure."

It's natural to shy away from people if you think they may try and push something on you that you don't want or need. Unfortunately, it can be too easy for someone to get into the financial services industry without a great deal of experience, align with a firm that puts them through a training program, and then go out with a business card that says Financial Advisor on it. It's important to understand there are designations and credentials that can be obtained, and to do so requires a much greater depth of knowledge and experience. Let's look at a couple of these in more detail.

Requirements for Practicing Medicine and Law vs. Financial Planning

Would you have a salesperson defend you in court or remove your spleen? If you want to become a medical doctor or a lawyer, then there is a prescribed (no pun intended) path for you to take with respect to your educational background and requisite standardized tests. At a minimum, you must have a four-year bachelor's degree with a solid GPA and then have a strong score on either the MCAT or LSAT standardized test, depending on whether you are applying to medical school or law school. Following graduation, you must pass medical boards or the bar exam. In the case of becoming a MD, you must even take it a step further by completing a residency before you can practice. The point is, you can't simply go to the hospital, have an interview, and then a couple weeks later be holding a stethoscope to a patient's chest. Similarly, you can't have an interview at a law firm, get hired, and then later that month be sitting second chair during a murder trial. Yes, this sounds absolutely ludicrous, and I would hope you agree with me 100%!

I find it fascinating that in this country we allow an individual to become a financial advisor without a specific training regimen, prerequisite college degree, and a requirement to pass an extensive board examination. If this were required, at the very least this would show an individual had some acumen and baseline proficiency to be a financial advisor. It's preposterous that this is not required and it has to change. Can you sense that I'm passionate about this? In the meantime, you can require the aforementioned background of your financial advisor by accepting nothing less than the CFP credential behind his or her name. A CFP® professional has shown that he has the background necessary to enter into the profession and is worthy of the moniker financial advisor or financial planner, which I will use synonymously. What exactly is a CFP® professional and why should you care?

CFP® Designee vs. "Financial Advisor"

"If they're not a CFP pro, you just don't know." This is the new ad campaign being run by the CFP Board, and I think it's brilliant. In one of the spots, a financial advisor individually talks to several clients over the course of the commercial and asks them if they would trust him and would they hire him to manage their financial affairs. They all nod yes and agree to move forward with him. He seems pleasant, professional, and looks the part, but then the truth comes out: he's actually a deejay and knows nothing about financial planning whatsoever! They flash back to when he had long dreadlocks that were subsequently cut off prior to filming the ad and show him spinning records with his headphones on; they are all dumbfounded. The ad does a great job of stressing the point that without the CFP credential, you simply do not know who you are dealing with. Too much is on the line financially to make this mistake.

Initial CFP Certification: A Brief Look Inside

So that you can appreciate the rigor involved in obtaining the CFP certification, I have listed the requirements to become a CFP® professional below. This information, verbatim, comes directly from the CFP Board's website:[1]

To become certified, you are required to meet the following initial certification requirements (known as the four Es):

- Education
- Examination
- Experience
- Ethics

These four components are briefly described below; subsequent sections of this Guide to CFP Certification provide detailed information about each component. While the CFP certification requirements may be changed from time to time, you will be expected to meet the requirements that are in place at the time you apply for the CFP Certification Examination.

Education

The first step to CFP certification is to acquire the knowledge required to deliver professional, competent, and ethical financial planning services to clients, as outlined in the major personal financial planning topic areas identified by CFP Board's most recent Job Analysis Study. CFP Board's coursework component requires the completion of a college-level program of study in personal financial planning, or an accepted equivalent (through Challenge Status or Transcript Review), including completion of a financial plan development (capstone) course registered with CFP Board. You must also have earned a bachelor's degree (or higher) from a regionally accredited college or university in order to obtain CFP certification. The bachelor's degree requirement is a condition of initial certification; however, it is not a requirement to be eligible to take the CFP Certification Examination and does not need to be met before registering for the examination. CFP Board does not grant equivalencies or exceptions to the bachelor's degree education requirement.

---

1 "CFP Certification Requirements," http://www.cfp.net/become-a-cfp-professional/cfp-certification-requirements.

Examination

After you have successfully met the education coursework requirement, you will be eligible to register for the CFP Certification Examination. The CFP Certification Examination assesses your ability to apply your financial planning knowledge, in an integrated format, to financial planning situations. Combined with the education, experience, and ethics requirements, it assures the public that you have met a level of competency appropriate for professional practice.

Experience

Because CFP certification indicates to the public your ability to provide financial planning without supervision, CFP Board requires you to have three years of professional experience in the financial planning process, or two years of apprenticeship experience that meets additional requirements. Qualifying experience may be acquired through a variety of activities and professional settings, including personal delivery, supervision, direct support, or teaching.

Ethics

CFP® professionals agree to adhere to the high standards of ethics and practice outlined in the CFP Board's Standards of Professional Conduct and to acknowledge CFP Board's right to enforce them through its Disciplinary Rules and Procedures. When you have completed the education, examination, and experience components of the CFP certification process, you will be directed to complete a CFP Certification Application on which you will be asked to disclose information about your background, including your involvement in any criminal, civil, governmental, or self-regulatory agency proceeding or inquiry, bankruptcy, customer complaint, filing, termination/internal reviews conducted by your employer or firm. CFP Board conducts a detailed background check for all candidates, including review of any disclosures made on the CFP Certification Application. Matters that may or will bar you from obtaining certification are investigated in accordance with CFP Board's Disciplinary Rules and Procedures. Authorization to use the CFP marks will not be approved until the background check and any investigation are concluded successfully.

Important Note

Applicants for CFP certification are required to satisfy the CFP Board's Fitness Standards for Candidates and Professionals Eligible for Reinstatement, which describe conduct that will always bar an individual from becoming certified and conduct that is presumed to be unacceptable and will bar an individual from becoming certified unless the individual successfully petitions CFP Board's Disciplinary and Ethics Commission for consideration. The CFP Board encourages all individuals pursuing CFP certification to review the Fitness Standards for Candidates and Professionals Eligible for Reinstatement before addressing the other certification requirements.

Proliferation of Professional Designations—How to Make Heads or Tails of the Alphabet Soup

There are literally over 165 professional designations out there. You can find a comprehensive list of them at www.Finra.org/investors/professional-designations. I have provided an overview of some of the common designations you may see and what they mean:

- **CFP (CERTIFIED FINANCIAL PLANNER™)**
  Issued by the CFP Board of Standards and the de facto financial planning credential, as explained above.
- **CPA (Certified Public Accountant)**
  Issued by the AICPA and the de facto tax advising credential.
- **CPA|PFS**
  A CPA with a PFS (Personal Financial Specialist) designation has been trained in financial planning.

- **CFA (Chartered Financial Analyst)**
  Issued by the CFA Institute and the de facto investment management designation.
- **ChFC (Chartered Financial Consultant)**
  Issued by the American College and connotes proficiency in financial planning. Similar to the CFP, but without the comprehensive Board exam component.
- **CLU (Chartered Life Underwriter)**
  Issued by the American College and the de facto life insurance designation.

I have served as a Subject Matter Expert for the CFP Board in developing test questions for the CFP Board Certification Exam. These sessions are rich in content, and I am always impressed by the amount of talent assembled in the room. All of the attendees are CFP® professionals and many are practicing advisors, while some are college professors and others work for nonprofits or in government positions. There is a methodical process that the CFP Board uses to develop test questions. I am only bringing up this subject because I want you to understand how difficult the exam can be, which even further substantiates my stance on why you need to work with a CFP® professional and accept nothing less. Historically, according to the CFP Board, the pass rate for first-time test takers ranges from 49% to 60%. The primary objective of the test is to ensure that the candidate, on the day of the exam, has a baseline proficiency in the body of knowledge determined by the CFP Board to be essential in being able to be designated as a CFP® professional. What do I mean by this? In practical terms, it means that when taking the six-hour exam a candidate may be faced with the following types of questions, back-to-back: a question that requires calculating the duration of a bond, followed by a question on which type of homeowner's policy would be the most appropriate given a set of facts, only to be followed by a complex estate tax calculation.

Knowing that your advisor has the CFP credential can give you greater confidence that he or she has the proven knowledge to help you with your FinLife® and to be your Money Navigator.

A Note on Advanced Education

I have already established that your financial advisor should hold the CFP credential, but should she also have a degree related to the field of financial planning and investments? My opinion on this is that it is not essential, but highly preferred. In addition to the CFP designation, if your advisor also has an undergraduate or graduate degree in financial planning, economics, finance, investments, tax, or accounting, this, in my opinion, is a huge plus, as their overall knowledge base and subject matter acumen oftentimes exceeds an advisor's who does not hold these degrees. At the end of the day, the advisor possessing an advanced degree can only help you as she brings more education, and thereby intellectual capital, to the table to assist you.

Emotional Core Concerns: Financial Advisor vs. CFP® Professional

In the book *Beyond Reason*, Roger Fisher and Daniel Shapiro provide the reader with a guide on how to understand your emotional core concerns. Your core concerns are feelings and do not require words to be felt or expressed. A skilled financial advisor who is a Money Navigator should be adept at practicing the five core concerns, particularly as they relate to working with clients. Next, I'll briefly discuss the five core concerns (Appreciation, Affiliation, Autonomy, Status, and Role) and how the Money Navigator would utilize them as part of establishing a meaningful, healthy, and impactful relationship with you.

Let's face it, we all want to be appreciated for who we are, aspects of our personalities, what we have accomplished or overcome, and our contributions to those around us. According to Fisher and Shapiro, *Appreciation* is a core concern that is ignored when someone diminishes or denigrates your way of thinking or your actions. You could liken this to a financial advisor being judgmental about investments you have made or the long-term-care insurance policy you have purchased prior to having engaged with her. You feel unappreciated as a result. Conversely, the Money Navigator acknowledges the merit of your thinking and the actions you have taken. The Money Navigator, instead of devaluing your existing investment portfolio and insurance purchase, may say something like, "You've made a wise move in attempting to diversify your assets with many different types of investment vehicles." Similarly, regarding your insurance purchase, she may say, "The long-term care insurance policy you purchased is quite expensive and may lack coverage in some areas, but it still can be equated with transferring a large potential risk to an insurance company for pennies on the dollar." We all feel appreciated when our opinions and actions are validated first. Our decisions may not always be optimal, but our defense mechanism goes into high alert if the first shot fired is laden with criticism. Validation is a good first step toward appreciation, a step that the Money Navigator knows well. If you feel validated, you feel appreciated and ultimately understood.

Most of us have an inherent desire to be part of something bigger than ourselves. *Beyond Reason* refers to this core concern as *Affiliation*. Lack of affiliation can occur when, for example, a financial advisor doesn't take the time to get to know you or understand the groups to which you belong on a professional and personal level. In the average financial advisor's mind, you may be just another client, a number, nothing more and nothing less. The Money Navigator, on the other hand, takes the time to truly understand you professionally and personally. This leads to deeper, more meaningful relationships built on trust. He may ask you about the groups with whom you are affiliated. Are you a member of the local Rotary chapter or church, for example? Why? Do you participate in certain industry functions for C-suite executives? Do you enjoy tennis or golf? Are you passionate about the theater? How did that come about? As a result of these interactions and conversations, you feel much better about the affiliation with the Money Navigator and his firm, and this makes you feel more like a colleague and not an outsider or adversary. Ultimately, if your affiliations are acknowledged, you feel more open to interacting with the Money Navigator.

According to Fisher and Shapiro, when your decision-making ability is hindered or quashed, your core concern of *Autonomy* is not being met. If your financial advisor makes trades in your account and doesn't ever explain to you why they were made and in the process takes on an aura of the omniscient expert, you may feel your autonomy is being infringed upon. The Money Navigator is a master communicator and makes sure that you are aware of why your account was traded in a particular way by keeping the lines of communication open and active. Additionally, the Money Navigator lays out the rules of the game well in advance so there are no surprises, which in turn provides you with confidence and clarity. If your autonomy is recognized by the Money Navigator, your likelihood of making meaningful progress with your FinLife® multiplies exponentially.

We all crave *Status* to a certain degree, whether via family, community, or work. For example, the financial advisor who operates on a surface-level basis may often miss the fact that you happen to be the president of the city's popular Bocce Club. This is a big deal to you, and you spend quite of bit of time, money, and energy on this endeavor. The Money Navigator knows that you are the president and, furthermore, he knows that you founded the local chapter and are on the National Bocce Club board of directors. The Money Navigator has acknowledged your status and as a result earned not only your business, but your friendship and, most importantly, your trust. Your status is central to who you are at your core, so why shouldn't it also be one of the items at the nucleus of your relationship with the Money Navigator in order for him to do the best job possible for you?

The fifth area is the *Role* you play. I'm sure you wouldn't like it if your role were trivialized or belittled, as this may upset you or make you feel diminished. The financial advisor who doesn't recognize that you are a part-time adjunct professor but have lost your passion for teaching psychology courses at the local community college has missed the boat on how you feel about one of your roles in life. In addition to the obvious roles of being an executive, parent, and spouse, you are also an educator. This was important to you at one time, but now this role is no longer personally fulfilling. The Money Navigator has elicited this information from you through rich and engaging dialogue during meetings with you. As a result, you feel more connected to the Money Navigator because he understands you at your core being. He realizes that one of your many roles is not currently fulfilling, and he can be a sounding board to help you with your decision making in this regard. Perhaps he helps you to disengage with the community college and begin writing a book on psychology instead. Being an author may be a much more fulfilling role for you. Your role in life is at the very essence of your being, so this point should not be played down. The Money Navigator values the various roles you play in your life and, as a result, assuages your worries and fears and instead builds confidence and reassurance of success.

Conversations and touch points with your financial advisor should be meaningful and the conversations poignant in content. The Money Navigator who understands your emotional core concerns and acknowledges them regularly represents a rarity in today's fast-paced, digitized, impersonal society. When you find this individual, do not let her go!

Again, think back to the barriers to entry issue I raised earlier. You don't want to be receiving your financial planning from a part-timer who is actually a deejay, do you? Additionally, as a result of the public demand for highly credentialed financial advisors, over the past five years or so there has been a proliferation of CFP Board–approved undergraduate and graduate programs. The public should demand more educational hurdles and credentialing for financial advisors. You can insist upon it by only hiring a real pro, a Money Navigator.

Chapter Takeaways

Cusp of Retirement

You're closing in on turn four in the NASCAR race of your working life. Just as you would rather have Jimmy Johnson or Dale Earnhardt Jr. behind the wheel driving you in the Daytona 500, you also desire to have a professional Money Navigator help you drive your FinLife® plan as you approach retirement. You certainly wouldn't let a NASCAR intern get behind the wheel with you, so why let someone who may actually be a deejay help you with this extremely important aspect of your life, your financial well-being? Instead, go to the CFP Board's website (www.cfp.net) and search for CFP® professionals who have the background, experience, and specialties you are looking for in an advisor. Then interview the top three to five of them and determine which one is qualified to be your Money Navigator. Don't accept anything less, because you certainly wouldn't put your life in the hands of a NASCAR intern, so why do the same thing with your FinLife®?

Already Retired

If you are like a lot of retirees with whom I work, you have grown up in a certain era where professionals were viewed as highly skilled and greatly accomplished in their respective areas of specialty. You appreciate the fact that doctors have had a significant amount of schooling, board examinations, and experience in order to be able to positively impact the lives of whom they come in contact. You also realize that lawyers have had prerequisite schooling, board exams, and associate-level experience requirements in order to practice law before the courts. On the financial advisory front, most of your experience with financial advisors has likely been from traditional stockbrokers at the large warehouse firms, which we discussed in chapter 6. You understand that your stockbroker likely has not passed the same educational hurdles as your lawyer or doctor, so perhaps you don't consider them as being on the same professional level.

As a retiree, just as you hire a doctor or an attorney based upon their credentials and experience, you should insist on hiring a true Money Navigator to help you with your FinLife®. This is an experienced CFP® professional who works as a fiduciary for an independent RIA and as a bonus has an advanced degree.

Facing a Life Transition

A couple faced an enormous life transition during a period of time that should have been the happiest in their lives. While in the process of becoming parents for the first time, tragedy struck when their child was infected in utero by a deadly bacteria. When the child was born, she was immediately taken to the neonatal intensive care unit, as her Apgar score[1] was a 1 on a scale of 1 to 10! Luckily she survived, but for years she was monitored for physical and neurological abnormalities, which ultimately never occurred. During this time, the couple ended up finding out what caused their child's sickness. It happened to be a contaminated food product that the mother had eaten during her pregnancy.

As a result of this finding, the couple filed a lawsuit against the food manufacturer, which had neglected to maintain cleanliness in their facilities, leading to multiple contamination outbreaks and many sick mothers and children, some who unfortunately died as a result.

Fast forward six years after the birth of their child, and the couple were awarded a legal settlement. The amount of the settlement certainly didn't make up for the fact that their daughter had been stricken ill before even being born, but it did help to assuage some of the concerns they had about the financial future for their child.

The Money Navigator guided them, along with their attorneys, through the process of negotiating and evaluating the eventual settlement and subsequently helped them invest the proceeds in the manner that provided the daughter with long-term security. Unfortunately, something like this could happen to you or a loved one, so it is imperative that you have a go-to individual, a Money Navigator, to assist you during such a difficult life transition moment.

---

1   Although the Apgar score was developed in 1952 by an anesthesiologist named Virginia Apgar, you also might hear it referred to as an acronym for: Appearance, Pulse, Grimace, Activity, and Respiration. The Apgar test is usually given to a baby twice: once at one minute after birth, and again at five minutes after birth. Dr. L. Hirsch (2014) "What Is the Apgar Score?" retrieved January 17, 2017, from http://kidshealth.org/en/parents/apgar.html.

The Money Navigator in Depth

"Even if you are on the right track, you will get run over if you just sit there."

— *Will Rogers*

CHAPTER 9

Talking With Your Money Navigator

"A leader is the one who knows the way, goes the way, and shows the way."
—John C. Maxwell

As I have discussed throughout this book, the world has clearly changed. Therefore, so must all of us. We can do better. If you are going on a sailing trip, do you simply chart the course and sail in a straight line? Of course not! When you sail, you realize that it is all but inevitable that the winds and currents will change, so you'll have to tack, or methodically zigzag back and forth, to take advantage of what Mother Nature is or is not providing you. When a storm brews, it may make sense to shorten the sails and take safe harbor in a port, or to drop anchor, batten down the hatches, and ride out the storm. Why should your FinLife® management plan be any different? When you're charting your course, whether it be with respect to sailing or your FinLife®, you will encounter times when you can be knocked off course and adjustments need to be made in order to ultimately reach your desired destination.

One thing is for certain in life, and that is that things will change. Therefore, your FinLife® plan needs to be able to change as well, and adjustments and course corrections are inevitable. By now I think you have figured out that the Money Navigator can be considered a safe harbor for his clients, and his process lasts long term. The safe harbor represents the one place you can bring all of your financial concerns. In this chapter, we'll discuss what you can expect from your meetings with a local advisor, including outlining basic measures of success, your happiness, your lifestyle goals, and your retirement goals. By gaining a better understanding of this relationship, that safe harbor will become more appealing—and within your reach.

Living Your Ideal FinLife®

The Money Navigator meets with you regularly, usually at least twice a year, but that can certainly vary. During these meetings your FinLife® plan is updated based upon the current market conditions, your new goals and objectives, law changes, tax provisions, or any life events that have occurred since the previous meeting. These new inputs enable your FinLife® plan to be stress-tested with many different variables and scenarios that you would like to see. This way your FinLife® plan is a living and breathing digital document that is dynamically adjusted based upon what is going on in your life and in the world. As a result, you feel engaged in the process, and the Money Navigator helps you to feel confident in your ability to live your Ideal FinLife®.

When initially meeting with you, the Money Navigator should ask you what your measurement of success is for a financial advisor. Would you prefer that your advisor manage investment returns or your wealth? In other words, what do you think you care more about: percentages, or overall dollars and making sound decisions? The answers the Money Navigator receives to these questions are interesting and telling about today's culture as well as your own unique lens with which you view the world. If performance really mattered, two people achieving the same returns should be equally happy, right? Unfortunately, this is far from the case, and here's why:

	Client A	Market Returns		Client B
Starting Value	$1,000,000	25%	-14%	$1,000,000
Year 1	1,150,000	35%	-12%	791,200
Year 2	1,444,500	12%	10%	625,856
Year 3	1,528,240	25%	6%	600,442
Year 4	1,810,300	21%	-8%	551,668
Year 5	2,093,663	-8%	21%	433,935
Year 6	1,852,570	6%	25%	428,261
Year 7	1,878,924	10%	12%	435,326
Year 8	1,978,817	-12%	35%	397,965
Year 9	1,670,959	-14%	25%	429,253
Ending Value	$1,368,224	10%	10%	$436,566

Same initial portfolio value ($1 million) and annual withdrawals ($80,000 per year).
Same time-weighted rate of return, different dollar-weighted ending wealth. Average rates of
return over a 10-year period, compound calculation.

Let's say you are Client A and your friend is Client B in the chart above. You both deposited $1,000,000 into an investment portfolio with an advisor and subsequently withdrew $80,000 per year to supplement your income. So as Client A you were extremely pleased with your advisor until the sixth year, when your portfolio declined from just over $2 million to about $1.85 million. Then your portfolio stayed level for a couple of years and then went down for the final two, resulting in a final ending value of $1,368,224. Meanwhile, Client B wasn't so fortunate, as his portfolio dropped precipitously until the seventh year, when it checked in at $435,326. He ended up at $436,566 in the tenth year, over $900,000 less than your portfolio's ending value. But you both average 10% for the ten-year period! How can this be? This is impossible, isn't it? Actually it is possible, and you'll see why in a second. If you look closely at the market returns column, you'll notice that there is a pattern to them. Client B's returns are simply your returns presented in reverse order. This is what we refer to as return sequencing. It means that the order in which investment returns occur in the real world can have dramatic ramifications.

Based upon what transpired, Client B is less than happy with his financial advisor, and it's highly unlikely that the advisor he began with is the advisor with whom he finished this ten-year journey. Interestingly, although you have almost $1 million more in portfolio value, you are unhappy as well. The reason is twofold: (1) when your portfolio was over the $2 million mark and all your goals could be confidently met with this amount of money, your financial advisor failed to make a course adjustment and de-risk the portfolio; and (2) humans remember the highest value that their portfolios ever attained and make judgments from there. The message here is clear—be careful about placing too much emphasis on rates of return.

The Money Navigator helps you measure success in three ways. First, to determine how you are doing with your FinLife® planning, he doesn't measure your plan against some random market index. Instead, the Money Navigator measures how you are doing relative to what matters to *you*— what it is that you value and are passionate about. He creates a funding score (a probability of success measurement), which provides you with clarity and confidence about your financial future. Second, the Money Navigator helps you determine your margin for error so you can determine how sensitive your plan's success is to forces that are beyond your control. Finally, if any changes need to be made (course corrections, if you will), how will those changes impact your hopes, goals, and dreams? This process is comprised of a trade-offs discussion that clearly outlines what you need versus what you want and what you need now versus what you need later.

You have five control factors that you can utilize to drive your FinLife® plan and ultimately your Ideal FinLife®. The first is the amount you *spend*. What kind of lifestyle do you want to support, and do you have the wherewithal financially to do so? Second, *savings* and excess cash flow dedicated for investment is something that you can control. The *timing* of your choices that involve your finances is the next control factor that you possess. We cannot control the markets, but we can control the volatility of our investment portfolios and therefore the amount of *risk* that we are undertaking. The last control factor is how much of a *legacy* you desire to pass on to your heirs or charitable causes. One thing you *cannot* control is the market, so don't attempt to do so.

The Money Navigator helps you to focus on the things you can control as opposed to becoming frustrated with or fearful of things that you simply cannot. He stays with you and tracks your funding score over time so you will know when you are on track or if you're not, that course corrections need to be made. You only have one life to live, and do-overs do not exist. The Money Navigator's primary objective is to help you live your life without the fear that you will run out of money, but just as important, not living so far beneath your means that you die on a mattress full of money you could (and should) have spent.

Why Happiness Matters

I recently had the opportunity to attend a talk that Shawn Achor, author of *The Happiness Advantage*, gave about the subject of happiness.[1] One of the unique things about Shawn, in addition to the twelve or so years he has spent at Harvard researching the subject of happiness, is his ability to make fun of himself, and he does it better than anyone. His self-deprecating humor makes you instantly feel connected to him and at ease even though he is speaking to literally hundreds of people in a room. There were several takeaways I got from his talk, and the first was that happiness is the joy you feel as you move toward your potential. Potential can be defined in many different ways, but what is important is what it means to you specifically. You might want to sing or become a published author or engage in thrill sports such as skydiving, and as you move toward your potential, even if you have not yet reached it, happiness is the result.

One of the greatest predictors of happiness is the belief that your behavior matters. Ideally you need to care about your behavior and how to be more aware of its impact on your decision making and choice architecture. If you take ownership of the idea that your behavior does, in fact, make a difference in the outcomes in your life, you will ultimately be happier. A strong social connection provides you with a higher likelihood of success. Think about it: If you need to bounce an idea off of someone who has "already been there and done that," wouldn't that be better than trying to reinvent the wheel? A strong social network can pay huge dividends toward your happiness and ultimately your success. Finally, perceiving stress as a challenge rather than an impediment or threat is critical, as stress is simply a part of life, so managing our reaction to it makes a monumental

---

1 S. Achor, "The Happiness Advantage," speech presented at United Capital Executive Summit, Laguna Beach, California, January 2016.

difference in our ability to be happy and feel accomplished.

One of the best things I gleaned from Shawn's talk was how to implement a Conscious Acts of Kindness (we call it the CAKe) program at my office. Every month, each of our employees has a $100 budget to spend on anything they want to for a client or clients. Suppose Mr. Smith called in and one of our employees helped him out with a wire transfer, and during the course of the call the employee learned that Mr. Smith's son made the varsity tennis team for his high school. Mr. Smith absolutely beamed with pride that his son accomplished this as a sophomore, particularly since the school is large and the tennis team is extremely competitive in the state. What's great about the CAKe program is, once the employee took care of the wire request and hung up the phone, he immediately had the option to order Mr. Smith a gift certificate from an online tennis shop so his son could buy a new racquet, tennis clothing, or pair of tennis shorts. This is a kind and human gesture that says not only does the Money Navigator provide great customer service, but he cares, his people listen well, actually hear you, and know what matters to you on a personal level. We enjoy focusing on happiness for our clients.

Home, Work, and Leisure—Graying Your Borders

In today's society, a lot of us are extremely pressed for time, overworked, stressed out, underpaid, unfulfilled, and therefore yearning for a semblance of order or peace. In the past, it was required that if you worked long hours, you sacrificed home life and would forgo leisure activities. It was black or white in context, binary, one way or the other. I would argue that due to technological advances, as long as you have a mobile phone and reliable Internet access, you can work from anywhere on the planet. That means you can be *where* you want to be *when* you want to be there doing *what* you want to do and *how* you want to be doing it. Now, yes, certain jobs require you to be present at the jobsite, but many do not, and that is where graying your borders comes into play.

Enter John Venn, an English mathematician from the late nineteenth and early twentieth centuries. His diagrams, now termed Venn diagrams, utilize a simplistic concept to show the interrelationships between ideas using overlapping circles. Take a look below at a Venn diagram that explains the graying of your borders concept.

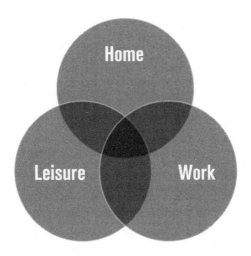

Carl Richards, a fellow author and CFP® professional, has taken the Venn diagram concept to an entirely new level by using a Sharpie pen to explain complex concepts succinctly. His book, *The Behavior Gap*, utilizes Sharpie/Venn diagrams and is a must-read. The book's primary premise is investor vs. investment returns, which I discussed in chapter 4.

If you are interested in graying your borders now, perhaps you should ask your financial advisor if she could show you how you could do so now as opposed to later. After all, life is short, so if you can gray today, why wait for later? This plays directly into the next concept, which takes graying your borders one step further—living your retirement lifestyle now!

Live Your Retirement Lifestyle Now

Why not retire now? Most people simply haven't realized that it is possible for them to retire early and lengthen their productive lives by many years. The bottom line is that there really isn't much information or education provided on the concept of true retirement, as I would define the phrase. What you often hear about is how individuals push themselves for decades in stressful jobs that they often are less than enamored with, all for the goal of getting to the magic age of sixty-five years old. Once arriving at sixty-five, they pull the pin on the career and move south for a life of the three Bs: beaches, boating, and bingo—or the permanent vacation.

There have been studies about people who have attempted to follow this road map, and what they show is a propensity for these folks to die prematurely, say five years prior to retirement, due to the massive amounts of stress, disappointment, and overall lack of personal fulfillment. Take a step back for a moment and think about how pushing yourself in a highly stressful environment for years, even decades, can take its physical toll upon you. Adding to this phenomenon is the fact that many individuals are inactive and do not regularly exercise but instead self-medicate with food, alcohol, drugs, and watching television or surfing the Internet. This creates a cycle of deterioration, as we are not built to be inactive for long periods of time. Additionally, we crave a sense of purpose, and being in an unfulfilling job for an extended period of time can be the death knell.

During a client (names and situation have been changed for confidentiality reasons) meeting the other day when the subject of living your retirement lifestyle now popped up, my client's wife started laughing out loud. She then nodded and said, "Bob has been doing this for years." Bob laughed and said perplexedly, "What in the world are you talking about, Mary?" Mary then said, "Seriously, you were in your pajamas until five thirty p.m. yesterday making deals on the phone, honey." It was as if she had caught him with his hand in the cookie jar, as he turned a bright shade of crimson. Bob is an extremely successful software salesman but just so happens to conduct work in his pj's many days, and why? Because he can! He can do this due to advances in technology, as all he really needs is a laptop, a mobile phone, and Internet access, and he can be anywhere conducting business anytime. I know a guy who holds conference calls between black diamond ski runs and during nature hikes. It can be done. Depending on how you structure your work circumstances, you can be living your retirement lifestyle now.

In my opinion, retirement should not be viewed as the permanent vacation at all. Instead, I'd like you take a different perspective and to think of retirement as a change in your career, whereby you are growing as a person and expanding your true passions. What's your passion? It may be starting a new business or consultancy, volunteering for a cause, or going on a religious mission. It may be something as simple as down-shifting a bit in your current capacity at work so you can spend more quality time with the family. Only you can define what's important to you about retirement.

I am convinced that if you do the following three things, you can set yourself up to be able to retire (again, this is not the permanent vacation, but the passionate career change or downshift) in your fifties. The first is keeping your lifestyle within reason and consumer debt at low levels. Nothing impinges more on your FinLife® than paying someone else for the privilege of borrowing their money. The second is being a good steward of savings through proper asset management. Finally, you should stay engaged in the FinLife® management process so you understand the ramifications of your decision making. Sound decisions yield a lifetime of good results.

If you are going to be spending up to one third of your life in retirement, staying engaged is more important than ever, which promulgates good health and therefore a prolonged quality of life. What exactly do I mean by staying engaged? It means different things to different people, but I have some suggestions for your consideration. Get involved in some volunteer work. Studies have shown that older adults who are involved in volunteering efforts live longer lives than those who opt out of this type of activity. Volunteers tend to enjoy better physical and mental health than their less active peers. Volunteerism promotes a sense of belonging, community, giving back, and promotes activity. There are so many causes out there that you could get involved in—it just comes down to finding one that ignites your passion. As a retiree, in this new definition, you bring so much to the table in the way of wisdom and life experience so younger generations benefit immensely regardless of your chosen area of endeavor.

How about taking a part-time job? Contrary to the belief that companies don't want older employees, many firms are specifically looking for older workers due to their innate abilities and relevant expertise. Some options to consider would be returning to your previous field in a consultative capacity or expanding your horizons into a completely new area in which you have an interest. Working has ancillary benefits in that it provides a social outlet, feelings of accomplishment and being valued, and the ability to impact a younger generation of employees. In this scenario, continuing to work on a part-time basis should be a choice, not a necessity to make ends meet, and your FinLife® Money Navigator can help you with how to do this.

Get that degree you always dreamed of. Going back to school is a wonderful thing to do in retirement. I had a client a few years ago who retired from the federal government, and he had always dreamed of obtaining a master's degree. Through FinLife® planning sessions, we were able to show him that going back to school was not only a possibility, but that he could attend his ideal university, which happened to be in the UK. There was a particular program with which he was enthralled, so I helped him figure out how to pay for the tuition, afford the flat in London, and bring his wife along for the wonderful journey. Needless to say, when I saw him after he returned from his studies a year later, he had an ear-to-ear smile and was so happy that he was able to fulfill a lifelong dream in retirement. Personally, I had a similar dream of obtaining a master's degree in finance and did so several years ago, while continuing to work full time, and then followed my master's up with a PhD in economics. Continuing my quest for continuing education, I'm currently pursuing a postdoctoral master's in applied analytics from Columbia University. Yes, I know I am not retired yet, but keeping the mind razor sharp is a great thing to do at all times, including in retirement. You may be saying you don't have time or the motivation to pursue a degree for one, two, three, or four years, and that is perfectly fine. What if you wanted to earn a certificate in a subject that interested you, or maybe you have the desire to audit a graduate class on English literature or ancient civilizations. Maybe you want to learn another language or take up playing the piano or guitar. Whatever your dream may be, go for it!

Your retirement may be closer in reach than you think, particularly with the way I have defined retirement. Just think for a moment about what your life would be like if you were doing what you have always wanted to do. Life is short. Don't wait; start the process of moving toward living your retirement lifestyle now!

You Can CHOOSE What You Want

As I said at the beginning of this chapter, change is inevitable, and it is especially so if you are beginning on your journey to FinLife® management. I have adopted Rachel Flower's methodology, which she calls the CHOOSE model,[2] and I utilize it with clients to promote richer

2 R. Flower, "The CHOOSE Model," lecture presented in Lake Tahoe, Nevada, May 2015.

conversations that result in deeper relationships and bottom-line results. CHOOSE stands for the following:

C is your "Current Reality"
H is the "Heart" of the matter
O is for your "Obstacles"
O is for you to take "Ownership"
S is the "Steps" needed
E is to "Execute" your plan

I like the model due to its ability to be massively impactful and change lives. The following section describes how the Money Navigator uses the model, which he incorporates over the course of two or three meetings.

When sitting down with you for the first time, the Money Navigator takes the time to understand your Current reality, the "C" in the CHOOSE model. The Money Navigator starts by asking you questions about your life in general, not just those related to your financial situation. One of the first questions he would ask you is, "What brings you here today?" Then, the Money Navigator just listens—without judgment or interruption. The Money Navigator probes deeper by asking questions such as, "What would give you a greater sense of control?" or "What's working/not working for you right now?" She might ask, "How is that impacting your relationship/health/financial situation?" and "How does that make you feel?" Yes, it actually sounds like you are going to see a shrink, right? I must confess I don't have a psychologist's chaise longue in my office, but today's financial advisor must be skilled not only in left-brain finance, but also in the nuances of behavioral finance, which are deeply rooted in psychology and require right-brain thinking to contextualize and understand.

So, back to our first interview. The Money Navigator's next question may be, "What do you think is out of control right now?" or "In what areas do you need a more balanced life?" She might also ask, "What makes you feel overwhelmed?" or "What areas of your life are too hectic for you?" The point of these previous questions is to let you talk so the Money Navigator can completely understand your current reality.

We are now up to the "H" in the CHOOSE model. After reviewing your Current reality, the Money Navigator wants to get to the Heart of the matter. During this part of the meeting, he addresses specific quality-of-life issues as well as tangible and conceptual goals.

"What would your life look like?" and "What matters most to you?" are a couple of questions the Money Navigator may ask. When you answer these questions, he might follow up with, "Why is that so important to you?" and then really listen to glean a clearer understanding of who you are and what you are trying to accomplish during your time on this planet. This flows directly into asking you, "What are your dreams for your business/life?" and "What do you love to do for your hobbies/pastimes/causes?" When you respond, he'd likely ask, "What do you love most about it?" and "Where would you like to be in 'x' years' time?" After you've had a chance to discuss this, the Money Navigator would probably say, "What are your goals?" and "How will you get there?" Then he can get more granular when he'd ask, "What would your typical day look like?" As I'm sure you can imagine, the dialogue during these sessions is rich in content and emotionally charged. Inevitably your passions will surface, and this can only help the Money Navigator be more effective on your behalf.

The Money Navigator utilizes something called choice architecture for the next letter of the CHOOSE model, which is "O" for Obstacles. Choice architecture provides different ways in which choices are provided to you and reviews the impact of the presentation on your decision making. Here's what I mean. To begin the exercise, the Money Navigator might help you paint a picture of what it is you want financially. It could mean retiring at age fifty-five with an income you can't outlive, for example. He then assists you in painting another picture of the future that you don't want. You can't retire at fifty-five or you run out of money at age sixty-eight, for one example. The Money Navigator would then ask you, "What is getting in the way of your goals?" The impediment is likely time, money, or other resources. "What do you feel is stopping you from doing this?" and "What obstacles are you dealing with?" Going another step further, "If you don't address the problem, what will life be like six months/one year/three years from now?" and "How will that impact your family/relationships/health/finances?" Finally, "How will that feel?" I call this the loss aversion chasm. What I mean by this is, envision point A where you are now. You need to cross over a footbridge to point C. Point C represents your plan being carried out and you arriving at financial independence or retirement or whatever other goal you may have.

Point B is well below the footbridge and represents the chasm where you would fall if you don't do the necessary things you need to do to get to Point C. As humans, we are naturally loss averse, so this exercise resonates with you and makes you realize that planning properly is the only way to go to attain true financial freedom and independence. I discussed loss aversion in chapter 2, so please review those pages to see how this section interrelates.

The second "O" in the CHOOSE model refers to Ownership. This corresponds to your commitment to the goals you have highlighted so far. This is an important part of the process because you need to take ownership of the challenges and problems you are facing, but even more notably you must take ownership of the changes you need to make in order to accomplish the goals you have articulated. She'll ask "bridge" questions to elicit answers and drive dialogue. This is done by digging deeper by asking emotional questions. "How do you *feel* about 'x'?" or "What do you love to do?" are a couple of questions she might use. Then she may ask, "What concerns you about 'y'?" "Why is that so *important* to you?" or "What do you *love* about 'z'?" The Money Navigator then asks validation phrases such as, "That's really important to you, isn't it?" "I can see that means a lot to you, doesn't it?" or, "It's clear that you love doing that, don't you?" When you are asked these types of validation questions, more often than not, you feel like the Money Navigator truly "gets" you because you know she was actively listening and understands your position.

The next letter is "S," which stand for Steps. This is where the Money Navigator lays out a financial roadmap for you of steps you need to take in order to move in the direction of your desired future. He develops a priority action list, or PAL, for you that clearly describes how you are doing and what needs to be done in various financial areas so no stone is left unturned.

Finally, the "E" stands for Execute, which is where reality begins and your plan is implemented. The execution phase of the relationship can be done all at once, but that is rarely the case, as I have found that less is more when it comes to implementation. This phase can take several months and up to a year to complete. Remember, planning is not an event; it is a process.

Complicated vs. Complex

Life is not complicated! If something is complex, it consists of many different and connected parts. This sounds similar to the definition for complicated, but alas, it is not even close. Here's why: The economy and your FinLife® plan are complex. They refer to a complex adaptive system that is impacted by outside factors that can elicit change. Shocks to the economy happen all the time and thereby change the economic landscape at will. The same could be said for your FinLife® management plan. Scientists that have studied complex adaptive systems use the word "agents" to describe the parts of a system that digest and acclimate their behavior to data that they receive about the system in which they reside, according to Eric Beinhocker in *Origin of Wealth*.[3] This has led to complexity economics becoming quite a burgeoning field for research.

Whereas traditional economics focused on rational agents and static systems of equilibrium, complexity economics is based upon real-life market dynamics where irrationality of the participants regularly appears. "So, what does this have to do with my FinLife®?" you may be thinking. Turns out, quite a lot. As Tony Robbins said in his book *Money: Master the Game*,[4] "complexity is the enemy of execution." This means you need to be aware of the right things in order to be able to avoid the wrong things. In this case, don't get wrapped up in complications when the real issue at hand is how you are going to effectively execute your FinLife® plan given life's complexities. Again, life isn't complicated; it is complex, and the Money Navigator can help you adapt to change because it is a necessary way of life. He can help you achieve simplicity beyond complexity.

---

3   E. Beinhocker, *The Origin of Wealth: Evolution, Complexity, and the Radical Remaking of Economics* (Boston: Harvard Business School Press, 2006).

4   T. Robbins, *Money: Master the Game: 7 Simple Steps to Financial Freedom* (New York: Simon & Schuster, 2014).

Chapter Takeaways

Cusp of Retirement

While meeting with your Money Navigator and discussing your retirement plans with him, you may be surprised to find that you're closer to your goal than you think. Even though you think you are five to ten years away from retiring, perhaps the concepts of graying your borders and living your retirement lifestyle now could come into play for you today. Take a step back for a minute and think about your current job and its requirements. Also, think about how your home is set up. Would it be conducive to work from home a couple days a week? Reflect on what it is that you really like to do with your own time, your leisure pursuits. Can these areas be melded? In many cases, I think the answer is undoubtedly a resounding "yes"! Why work yourself to death, literally, all for the goal of retiring, if you can improve upon your overall quality of life by combining your home, work, and leisure activities today? You should go back and reread the CHOOSE model a few pages back so it resonates with you. Using the CHOOSE model with a Money Navigator can be a true difference maker in your ability to retire on your terms and time. This is critical when you are closing in on the big day. Don't waste another day without it!

Already Retired

It may be time to restructure your portfolio in retirement if your financial plan is overfunded. What I mean by overfunded is if you have enough money to live your Ideal FinLife® as you've defined it, it's likely time to de-risk your portfolio. As an example, if you are currently 80% invested in the stock market and 20% in the bond market and you have the resources necessary to achieve all of your goals, then it would be time to lower your equity exposure to 50%, for example. This prevents a bear market from negatively impacting your portfolio to the point of you having to adjust your goals downward. The proactive nature of the Money Navigator will help you to realize that it is time to de-risk your holdings, and this pragmatism can pay off for you and the probability of success of your financial plan.

Facing a Life Transition

Say you just had a newborn child in the past year. Congratulations! Needless to say, this represents a big transition. You are now not only concerned for your own health and well-being, but you have created a life that you are responsible for! How does a child impact your FinLife®?

Meeting with your Money Navigator and discussing this transition will help you focus your goals and determine where you need to be headed. Add your child to your health insurance plan, and it's a good idea to fill out the paperwork in advance. Check at work if there is a dependent care benefit that you can sign up for pretax. It's never too early for estate planning, so make sure you update your will to reflect guardianship issues. Make sure you and your significant other (if you have one, of course) have sufficient life insurance. Ensure that you have adequate income to cover the new increases in costs, because babies are not free! You should continue to save for your retirement because that day will still eventually come, but only if you plan. Of course you'll want to set up a college savings plan, but only after, I repeat, after you have set up a retirement savings plan. Consider moving to a bigger home in a better school district. Continue to make deposits into your relationship—make sure you have "date nights" now and then to continually invest in your relationship.

CHAPTER 10

The Money Navigator: You Can't Afford to Live Without One!

"Progress is impossible without change, and those who cannot change their minds cannot change anything."
—*George Bernard Shaw*

Jonathan Haidt wrote in his book *The Happiness Hypothesis*[1] that your brain is made up of two distinct sides. His vision is not unlike what we discussed in an earlier chapter, when we outlined the differences between right- and left-brain thinking. Haidt envisions these sides as the intuitive and the reflective. He uses an Elephant to represent the former and its Rider to represent the latter. In other words, the Elephant is your emotional side and the Rider is your rational side, which attempts to control the Elephant.

As we have discussed previously, we know that the vast majority of decisions are based upon emotion rather than logic. This disproportionality is perfectly analogized by the sheer size and magnitude of the Elephant versus the Rider. The Money Navigator knows that it is extremely difficult for the Rider to control the Elephant, who has not only tremendous size, but also much greater energy than the Rider. Think about this concept with respect to your FinLife®. For example: Let's say you

---

1 J. Haidt, *The Happiness Hypothesis: Finding Modern Truth in Ancient Wisdom* (New York: Basic Books, 2006).

desire to retire at a certain age and in order to do so you know that you need to contribute the maximum to your 401k, but you procrastinate because you'd rather be able to spend more money now on consumption. Changing this dynamic is not easy.

Incidentally, Shlomo Benartzi, PhD, of UCLA, has written a great book called *Save More Tomorrow*,[2] which reviews in detail the issue of committing now to invest future pay raises into your 401k plan. What happens often in reality is, instead of the Rider reining in the Elephant in order to invest in your 401k, the Rider fails and your retirement is now put in jeopardy. The Elephant wins and is instantly gratified by spending your hard-earned dollars on the latest gadget or taking an extravagant vacation on a whim. There needs to be a way that the Rider can keep the Elephant on the road to your retirement long enough to truly make a positive impact. To accomplish this, you need to be able to make sacrifices today in order to live your Ideal FinLife® in the future. This, however, must be balanced with the fact that the Rider likes to really think things through, sometimes to the point of paralysis by analysis as we reviewed earlier. There must be a way to balance the short-term thought process of the Elephant with the longer-term focus of the Rider.

The first step when encountering change is to appeal to your logical brain, or the Rider, by providing clarity regarding the change needed; so in this example it would mean contributing sufficiently to your 401k so that you can retire on your terms as you have defined them. Next, the process must appeal to your emotions because they are going to be the predominant force that drives the decision-making process. In this context, it could mean the Money Navigator using aging software on a photograph of yourself so that you can see what your future self looks like. If you've never seen this software, this may seem like a bizarre concept, but this exercise enables you to not only see how you would look but feel what you would feel if your retirement was unfunded, due to a lack of contributions over the years prior to the picture being taken. Again, this part of the exercise appeals to your emotions—the Elephant. The final piece of the process is having you visualize the road to your goal. In their best-selling book *Decisive*, Chip and Dan Heath call this "Shaping the

---

2   S. Benartzi, *Save More Tomorrow: Practical Behavioral Finance Solutions to Improve 401(k) Plans* (New York: Penguin, 2012).

Path," and a large part of this is helping you realize how things would be if you didn't contribute to your 401k. The concept of the Disproportionate Pain Trap comes into play in this regard, as it is a necessary component in order to motivate the Elephant to be reined in by the Rider so you move correctly down the road and don't fall into the chasm of failure or the loss-aversion chasm. The chasm of failure in this case is an underfunded plan for your ideal retirement. When the Rider realizes that this chasm exists, he can overpower the Elephant so your long-term goals can be achieved.

Your Money Navigator adds incredible value to your FinLife®: not just in terms of money, but also in terms of how you view your lifestyle options. In this chapter, I'll outline the concrete monetary benefits as well as the soft benefits of working with a Money Navigator.

The Ultimate Value Add

How much of an enhancement to your overall financial well-being can you expect when working with a Money Navigator? Vanguard performed a study in 2001 and again in 2014 on this very topic entitled "Putting a Value on Your Value: Quantifying Vanguard Advisor's Alpha."[3] The idea of the research was to figure out how much additional value advisors can add (Advisor's Alpha) by providing financial planning, behavioral coaching, and overall guidance (in other words, FinLife®!) within the context of a client relationship, instead of attempting to simply "beat the market." Additionally, Morningstar produced a report in 2013 built on their own research entitled "Alpha, Beta and Now... Gamma."[4] Morningstar uses the term Gamma somewhat synonymously with Advisor's Alpha. The findings of both reports were nothing short of extraordinary.

According to Vanguard and Morningstar, there are between five and eight primary areas where the Money Navigator can quantifiably add value or advisor's alpha to your FinLife®. The value-adds are measured in basis points ("bps"), or 1/100th of 1%, so for example, 25 bps is .25%.

3   F. Kinniry, CFA; C. Jaconetti, CPA, CFP; M. DiJoseph, CFA; and Y. Zilbering, "Putting a Value on Your Value: Quantifying Vanguard Advisor's Alpha" (Rep. Vanguard Research, 2014).
4   D. Blanchett, CFA, CFP, and P. Kaplan, PhD, CFA, "Alpha, Beta and Now... Gamma" (Rep. Morningstar Investment Management, 2013).

The first area where the Money Navigator can add value is by recommending an *asset allocation strategy* that aligns with your goals, objectives, time frames, and risk tolerance [total value-add is > 0 bps]. The second is by implementing *cost-effective investment solutions* by focusing on keeping expense ratios low. In other words, the Money Navigator pays close attention to your hurdle rate, or the amount the account needs to earn before you start making money! This is worth 45 bps on average.

The third is by utilizing a *rebalancing strategy* so the integrity of the investment allocation is maintained over time. It doesn't make that much of a difference whether this is done quarterly or annually, just that it is, in fact, done consistently [total value-add = 35 bps]. The fourth and, in my opinion, the most important is for the Money Navigator to utilize *behavioral coaching* as part of his modus operandi. Helping clients manage their emotions is *the* critical component of value-add during difficult times [total value-add = 150 bps]. Vanguard determined this by studying actual client behavior measured by investors who strayed from their initial allocation (chasing returns without factoring in risk) in retirement who lagged the benchmark by 150 bps. Other research has also concluded that behavioral coaching can enhance net returns by up to 200 bps!

The fifth is tax management and *asset location*. This ensures that your investments are placed into the correct account from a tax perspective. Think bonds or income-generating investments in IRAs and capital growth–oriented vehicles in taxable accounts [total value-add = 0 to 75 bps]. Spending strategies, or what I would term *distribution phase advising*, is the sixth area where the Money Navigator can add value [total value-add = 0 to 70 bps]. The seventh area is *total return versus income investing*. This helps you not only increase your income but also lower your taxes, as capital gains rates are paid when assets are sold to fund income needs [total value-add = > 0 bps]. The final area is implementing *guaranteed income strategies utilizing annuity allocations* [total value-add = 90 bps]. By hedging away longevity risk (yes, we are all living much longer these days), these strategies remove the fear of running out of money from the retirement equation.

After tallying up the bps for each area where the Money Navigator adds value, you arrive at approximately 3% to 4% value-add over not having him onboard. Let's just call it 3% for the sake of argument and to be conservative. It is important to realize that the 3% figure does not mean each and every year the Money Navigator will provide a 300 bps increase in return over what you would have achieved on your own. What happens in reality is the 3% occurs in lumps or can be bunched up, so to speak. The overriding message—there is unquestionable quantifiable value that the Money Navigator brings to the table!

The Money Navigator Is Vital, Given the Current Market Backdrop

As of this writing, the financial markets are clearly overvalued by most metrics you consider. We are in the middle of what I would call *the* unprecedented financial experiment being conducted by the Federal Reserve and central banks across the globe. Although the Fed has taken its foot off of the gas pedal (stopped printing money), other central banks (European Central Bank, Bank of England, and the Bank of Japan to name a few) are printing money like they never have in the past, and the financial markets are being stoked as a result. The Fed's balance sheet and the S&P 500 have been moving in lockstep, when normally they are negatively correlated. A bubble in equities has occurred and been caused by QE (Quantitative Easing, or money printing). I have no idea how long this will last, but one of two things will likely happen. At some point fundamentals will bring the market back down to logical valuations so it more closely aligns with the current economic growth plane (which is no great shakes) or the economy will improve enough to catch up to the overvalued market growth plane.

We are clearly at a crossroads in the global economy and financial markets. Now more than ever, it is important to have a Money Navigator assisting you with your investment portfolio. This is because diversification as we know it has been flipped on its head as asset classes that were noncorrelated in the past are now exhibiting significant correlation. More importantly, much of the correlation occurs on an "underwater" basis. What I mean by this is when markets are going down, the last thing you want is for the various asset classes in your investment portfolio to move together in lockstep. But that is exactly what is occurring when assets are correlated underwater. Increased connectivity of the global economy and financial markets is responsible for this phenomenon. This means that you need to be extremely discerning about what you are investing in and where, now and going forward.

Not too long ago, I happened to see economist Roger Arnold conduct a presentation about where the world is economically.[5] His theories warrant particular attention given their boldness. For the past forty-plus years the economies of the globe have been operating under four primary tenets: energy, technology, debt, and demographics. What exactly does Roger mean and how does it relate to you?

Oil consumption has supported "uneconomic" growth (i.e., expensive oil) for decades. Developing technology, debt, and demographics have counter-weighted oil's impact on the economies of the globe. There have been three areas of growth that have been counteracting expensive oil. Specifically, new technologies have spurred economic efficiencies, debt instruments have provided capital for economic growth and expansion, and demographics (primarily the aging baby boomers) have provided ever-increasing purchasing power.

Energy is everywhere, and two primary forces are at work: exergy and entropy, terms used in thermodynamics. Thermodynamics is a subject within the science of physics that is related to energy. Exergy brings *order* into the mix, while entropy provides *disorder*. To this point, for the past four decades, energy has been entropic. During this time debt was used as an exergetic force to counter the entropy of energy. Debt is now at peak levels on a global basis, so it is no longer exergetic; in fact, it has become entropic. An example of how bad this has gotten is the fact that Ireland recently issued a one-hundred-year bond, which essentially was a default or work-out loan because their sovereign debt levels had simply gotten too high.

Demographics also have been exergetic, balancing forces against high energy prices. That has begun to change because the baby boomers are aging and are flowing through the economy like a pig in a python. Peak consumption age occurs around fifty-four, so demographics are becoming entropic.

This leaves but one exergetic force: technology! Countries and companies need to increase technology development and innovation in order to

5   R. Arnold, "Energy, Technology, Debt and Demographics," speech presented at Rotary Breakfast Meeting, Great Falls, Virginia, November 2016.

combat the other three now entropic, disorderly tenets: energy, debt, and demographics.

So what does this mean with respect to your FinLife®, or more specifically your portfolio allocation? In the context of Mr. Arnold's thesis above, it means that the Money Navigator knows your portfolio allocation should consider the four tenets and their metamorphosis over the past four decades. Past, in this case, is likely not to mean prologue. In other words, investment returns will likely not be fueled by the same tenets that fueled them in the past. Allocating your portfolio accordingly is essential.

I recently was fortunate enough to hear Allianz economist Mohamed El-Erian speak about the current global economy and financial markets. His discussion was quite profound, and he said that we are at a point that he calls the "T-Junction" in his new book, *The Only Game in Town: Central Banks, Instability, and Avoiding the Next Collapse.*[6]

El-Erian contends that we are currently traveling down the road toward the T-Junction. The T-Junction is somewhat similar to the all-too-familiar "fork in the road" metaphor; however, by definition, a forked road could literally have more than two distinct ways to turn. What El-Erian means by the T-Junction is that we will truly be faced with a bimodal distribution instead of a normal distribution with several proverbial prongs in the fork. A bimodal distribution looks like a Bactrian (two humps) camel's back, whereas the normal distribution looks like a dromedary (one hump) camel's back, or the familiar bell curve. The reason this is important in this regard is because the idea connotes that there are but two alternatives of how things could play out on the world's economic stage. The two turns, left and right, involve two completely opposing outcomes. Simply put, we will either have renewed global economic growth and stability or be faced with economic stagnation and instability, according to El-Erian. Due to uncertainty, it is probably not a good idea to place large bets on either outcome because it's still too early in the economic game to make the call on what will eventually happen.

In the meantime, it is *not* the time to be paralyzed by uncertainty nor is it appropriate to back the truck up to the "big box equity store" and load up on stocks without a tactical overlay strategy in place (I discussed

---

6   M. A. El-Erian, *The Only Game in Town: Central Banks, Instability, and Avoiding the Next Collapse* (New York: Random House, 2016).

tactical investment strategies in chapter 5). To be clear, it is also not the time to run away from the market because you are fearful. It *is* the time to be extremely discerning about where you are currently investing so if we have the great sell-off, you are tactically protected against it, and on the other hand, if we have a continued market climb, you'll get the proverbial bite of the apple. In addition to tactical, I would consider adding in FIA exposure and alternative investments to provide downside protection, growth, income, absolute returns, and negative correlation. Alternatives can provide the "zig" you need when the markets "zag." The use of tactical methodologies, FIAs, and alternative investments provide you with what Dr. El-Erian says is needed in investment portfolios given the current market backdrop: (1) Resilience, (2) Agility, and (3) Optionality. Tactical provides you with Agility, FIAs provide you with Optionality, and Alternatives provide you with Resilience. Pretty tough trifecta! Now, let's take a look at each of the trifecta's components as they relate to your portfolio planning.

Resilience

Resilience refers to the ability to be flexible and to bounce back, or the capacity to recover quickly from difficulties. Merriam-Webster defines it as toughness. As it relates to your portfolio, resilience is nothing different, and alternative investments can provide you with this characteristic. Alternative investments can provide enhanced diversification, absolute returns, and negative correlation. Alternatives can act like a life preserver and provide *portfolio buoyancy* during times of market stress. For that reason, alternatives can play an integral role going forward given the current state of the markets. Hedge funds are considered alternative investments but can often be mischaracterized as risky assets. Some hedge funds, for example, are clearly risky; however, many others are structured as volatility dampeners designed to provide positive (or absolute) returns in all types of markets. Other alternatives that could be considered are master limited partnerships, real estate investment trusts, catastrophe bond and reinsurance portfolios, consumer debt portfolios, and life settlements. Your Money Navigator can assist you with evaluating these types of instruments to determine which one(s) make the most sense for you.

Agility

As humans, we are agile if we can be nimble and have the ability to quickly change direction. With respect to your investments, being agile connotes a similar meaning in that your portfolio needs to be able to be deft to adjust or change course when the situation dictates. This implies that your portfolio should have a tactical component, whereby the portfolio adjusts depending upon the current economic environment, momentum in the markets, interest rate trends, or financial stress indicators. Most tactical strategies are not meant to be predictive—rather, they're meant to be quickly reactive to the current applicable indicators. Tactical strategies are not considered market timing because these strategies are not simply moving money into cash when you are fearful and guessing when it is safe to put your toe back in the investing pond. With tactical strategies, you move from out-of-favor asset classes into more appropriate asset classes given the signals received (by the portfolio manager), which establishes a positional output—bullish, bearish, or neutral—and then adjusting accordingly at set intervals (usually weekly or monthly). The bottom line: Tactical strategies provide protection against severe bear markets! Your Money Navigator has done the appropriate due diligence to find the best available tactical money managers for you to use as part of your overall asset allocation plan.

Optionality

Options can provide you with choices and hope. Optionality as it relates to your investments is similar but provides you with upside potential (theoretically unlimited) with limited downside (if any). As I have discussed in chapter 7, Fixed Index Annuities provide you with optionality, as they give you upside potential in the market based upon an index (S&P 500, Nasdaq 100, Russell 2000, Barclays U.S. Dynamic Balance, etc.) and provide complete downside protection. There is no free lunch in life or with FIAs, but this makes complete sense because you are giving something up in order to get something else that you value. What I mean by this is although your principal is completely protected from any market losses, your returns are capped on a monthly or annual basis, so you do not receive the full upside of the market. Not a bad price to pay to be able to sleep at night.

The Trifecta Advantage

By utilizing a combination of alternative (resilience), tactical (agility), and fixed index annuity (optionality) strategies in your portfolio construction process, you are setting yourself up for success going forward given today's uncertain global economy and financial markets. I'm often asked what the ideal combination of these assets is, and I always say the same thing: "It depends." It depends upon who you are as an investor, your time horizon, goals and objectives, and your tolerance for risk. Similar to a London haberdasher who tailors a custom-made suit for his client, the Money Navigator knows to create a bespoke portfolio that fits you like a glove.

Chapter Takeaways

Cusp of Retirement

As you approach your retirement, this is clearly a time to be shrewd about where you invest your hard-earned funds. You have too much on the line, given how close you are to the finish line, to make a bad move now. The last thing you want is to fall victim to sequence-of-returns risk. Given this and the current state of the markets and global economy, you need to have the Trifecta Advantage working for you in full force. Make sure that you bring the tenets of tactical management, alternative investments, and fixed index annuities into the mix in an allocation commensurate with your risk tolerance so you have a portfolio that can weather any storm that should arise.

Already Retired

During your retirement, you should do your best to control the things you can control and not worry about the things you cannot. You can expend a lot of time and wasted energy fretting over uncontrollable events or issues, so know when to say when. Don't get sucked into the media frenzy spreading the economic *crisis du jour*. Specifically, you have the ability to determine how much you *spend* and *save* as well as the *timing* (for the most part) of the decisions you make financially. Ultimately you will decide how much *risk* you undertake and as a result what type of *legacy* you will leave for your heirs and causes to which you are dedicated. Being aware of these five control factors is a big step in the right direction of living your Ideal FinLife®.

Facing a Life Transition

Suppose you are facing a long-term care illness in your family. It could be that the illness is affecting your spouse or even a parent. The process of navigating a long-term care illness can be stressful from a logistical standpoint. If the individual is receiving home care, then coordinating caregivers, scheduling meals, doctor's visits, therapy sessions, medications, insurance claims, respite care, social visits, and housekeeping services all come into play. If nursing home care is the result, just about all of the above issues are necessities, as well as finding an acceptable facility, which requires a due diligence process in and of itself. Finally, who pays for the care? Private health insurance does not pay for long-term care expenses. Medicare does not pay for long-term care costs. Medicaid does pay, but only after you have become destitute by meeting a low financial threshold.

Long-term care insurance can be the logical stop-gap for this problem. LTC insurance covers all of the aforementioned costs (primarily classified as custodial care) so you do not have to come out of pocket for these expenditures, which can range from $60,000 to $150,000+ per year, depending upon where you live.

Keep in mind that LTC planning should be part of an overall FinLife® plan. Planning is not an event, so the same is true with the LTC component of your plan. Your policy should be reviewed annually by the Money Navigator to ensure it is the best plan at the best price for your particular situation.

Epilogue

This is unquestionably a critical time in history where planning your FinLife® is paramount. Gone are the days where you could simply use old rules of thumb such as "100 minus your age equals your equity exposure," set it, and then forget it. To be sure, your FinLife® is far more involved than that. As you've read the chapters in this book, I hope this fact has resonated with you. For those of you who are close to retirement, already retired, or facing a life transition, something more is needed, or more appropriately, *someone* is required for you to be able to assimilate the bombardment of data you face on a daily basis and conceptualize the information so it makes sense for you. In the labyrinth of choices you confront each and every week, it is essential to have a clearly defined personal decision matrix so you optimize your choice architecture. If you are operating at full efficiency and vigor in your work, leisure, and home life, it is imperative that you are self-aware of the fact that you must be truthful with the person staring back at you in the mirror and admit that you simply do not have the mental bandwidth to take on the complexities of your FinLife® planning effectively and impactfully in a DIY capacity. As we've reviewed in the book, you certainly don't perform surgery on yourself! Delegating this task to a capable and credentialed Money Navigator who is a resonant leader is essential so you can feel confident in your ability to achieve all of your FinLife® goals. Remember, you can live your retirement lifestyle today if you so desire. You need to work with a Money Navigator to progressively and continually tilt the odds of being successful in your favor. It is my sincere hope that in this book I've provided you with the necessary tools to do just that. Happy hunting!

Appendices

Real Life FinLife®

One of the most critical messages I hope you've come to understand after reading this book is that better decisions are often far more impactful on your FinLife® than investment returns. In other words, making sound decisions regarding the five control factors of spending, saving, timing, risk, and legacy will enhance the ability of your FinLife® plan to become reality more than any investment return ever will. In this appendix, you'll find concrete examples of how to put your new understanding into practice and make better decisions as you approach retirement, during your retirement, or when you are facing a life transition. Hopefully you can relate to some of these, as you may have faced or currently face similar situations or issues. Categorized into five sections (Employment, Family, House and Home, Money Management, and Retirement), each example below outlines a common situation requiring a smart decision and addresses how the knowledge you've gained in this book—along with the advice of a Money Navigator—can help you make the right choice.

Employment

Going Back to School

Expanding mental acuity, continuing education, satisfying an employment requirement, getting a promotion, following a lifelong passion for learning—any of these topics could be the reason you desire to go back to school. If you are considering going back to school, you'll need to make sure that this is a realistic undertaking from both a time and money perspective.

Real Life FinLife®
Remember the example I gave you in chapter 9 about the client who ended up going back to a university in London to obtain a master's degree after a long career in government? He was passionate about continuing his studies and he wanted to "check the box" on his quest to have a graduate degree in the field of horticulture. The Money Navigator can help you evaluate the trade-offs regarding following your educational pursuits.

New Job or Career

Embarking on a career change or starting a new job are exciting undertakings. At the same time, these can sometimes be risky moves, so reference points and third-party reviews are helpful as part of the evaluation process. Perhaps you've considered making the move because you are being offered a raise, an increase in responsibility, or in the case of changing careers, an opportunity to follow your true calling in life. Regardless of why you are thinking about making a change, it is important to evaluate your benefits package, your employment contract, and your compensation package before jumping headfirst into the position. This can enable you to conduct what-if scenarios based upon what is being offered to you, which in turn, provides you with the ability to evaluate the new job's impact on your FinLife® plan.

Real Life FinLife®
Jeff had been with the same telecom company for over twenty years, been paid well, and been given a significant amount of responsibility in his position. He came to us with an employment proposal from his company's biggest competitor. As his Money Navigator, we assisted Jeff by evaluating the proposed comp package and its resultant impact on his FinLife® plan. He did this by conducting a sensitivity analysis on the compensation plan utilizing a low, likely, and high total income approach in order to show the range of possible outcomes for Jeff. Additionally, the new job required that Jeff travel twice a month to another city two hours away via airplane. This brought a qualitative evaluation into the mix, as he would be required to be away from his family six to eight nights a month. Discussions evolved about how this would impact his relationship with his two high school daughters and whether it was worth it to not be around as often

during their formative years. In the end, Jeff ended up taking the new position because he felt that he had looked at the issue from several different
angles and became comfortable with the pros over the cons.

Employee Benefits Packages

There are an overwhelming number of choices out there when it comes
to evaluating the benefits you have from your employer. To name a few:
health insurance, dental, vision, life insurance, short and long-term disability insurance, long-term care insurance, deferred compensation, stock
options, restricted stock units, 401k plans, and beneficiary designations.
Making sense of it can be challenging, and the company benefits webinar
usually doesn't answer all of the questions you may have.

Real Life FinLife®
Allocating a client's 401k is one of the most common issues the Money
Navigator assists with as he builds out a client's FinLife® plan. We had a
client, Jim, who is like many employees—he didn't want to sign up for his
company 401k plan. Obviously this was a big mistake, since Jim's savings
are added pretax and grow tax deferred, but even more importantly, his
contributions were matched up to a certain percentage by his employer.
This is free money. Jim later decided to set up his 401k, but he initially
selected an allocation (sometimes recommended as the default allocation
by the company depending upon his age) and would likely not look at it
again for literally years. This is the "set it and forget it" method, and it
is exactly what clients should not do. To fix the situation, we integrated active management (fund due diligence, rebalancing, and allocation
changes) of Jim's 401k into Jim's overall FinLife® plan.

Starting a Business

Millions of small businesses are started each and every year. In fact, small
businesses are the backbone of the nation's economy. The majority of
small businesses will fail within the first two years. The primary reason
for this is poor planning or no planning at all. Whether you are open-
ing a restaurant, retail shop, or service-based consultancy, having a business plan is essential in order to improve your odds of success. There are

standard business plan templates that you can find on the Internet, and that is a great place to start. The other thing many small businesses fail to do at the onset is to get an unbiased set of eyes on the situation. Have someone who doesn't have a vested interest in the business take a look at the plan and provide you with advice. Of course, the person you select should have some experience in this area so the advice you receive is applicable and comes from a knowledgeable source.

Real Life FinLife®

Starting a new business can be exhilarating. This is what Tabitha thought when she decided that a hardware store was needed in her neighborhood. She was a successful marketing executive who had left the corporate world several years previously to start her own marketing consulting company. She wanted to become a franchisee of a national hardware store chain. Her rationale was quite simple. She felt that she could append to a going concern and start making money fairly quickly because there were no other hardware stores in her town. Having a national chain that had already developed a business plan seemed to be the way to go, and it required a total investment of $500,000 to $1,000,000.

Over the course of a couple of meetings and some phone calls, Tabitha and her Money Navigator arrived at the following conclusions. In order for the franchise to become a success, she would have to either work full time at the new store or hire an experienced manager. Did Tabitha want to quit her current job or be responsible for hiring and managing a store manager? Additionally, before embarking on the venture, a market study would need to be conducted on her local area to assess the viability of a new hardware store. After all, Home Depot and Lowe's stores were within seven miles of the town. Finally, what impact would the investment into the business have on her financial scorecard should the investment not pay off at all, do okay, or pay off well? In other words, what-if scenario testing was needed.

Ultimately, through continued dialogue with the Money Navigator, Tabitha decided against the franchise opportunity even though it passed the last two conclusions above (market viability study and the impact on her financial scorecard). The bottom line was that she was too engaged in her successful marketing consultancy to walk away from it or to oversee a manager of the proposed hardware store.

Selling a Business

This is your life's work. You have poured every ounce of energy, literally your heart and soul into your business, and now someone or some entity wants to buy it. This is exhilarating and nerve-racking at the same time! There are many questions you will have and want to ask. Is the offer even fair? What are my responsibilities going forward? Will I have to work with the new owners? If so, will we get along? Do I even want to sell right now? The list goes on and on.

Real Life FinLife®
Mario started his software development business with his good friend, Peter, fifteen years ago out of Mario's basement. The company specializes in developing software applications for the government to use for evaluating defense contractors. The government contracts that the company procured consistently increased in volume and dollar amount every year for the past ten years. The firm went from having two employees to over seventy-five and is a multimillion-dollar enterprise. When Mario was approached with a letter of intent (LOI) to purchase his company, it came out of thin air. He wasn't even considering selling, but the value of $30 million for the purchase price was eye-opening to say the least.

After getting over the initial shock, the first thing he did was enlist the help of his Money Navigator, who just so happened to have evaluated and advised on several of these types of transactions in the past. He helped Mario and Peter determine if the price was fair and if there were any financial caveats of which to be aware. One of the requirements of the transaction was a five-year consulting contract, which the Money Navigator thought was excessive, so it was negotiated down to three years. Additionally, the down payment was listed at 20% in the LOI, which in the Money Navigator's opinion was too low, so this was negotiated to a more reasonable and industry-standard 33%.

Ultimately, both Mario and Peter received pre- and post-transaction planning assistance from the Local Navigator. The pre-transaction guidance was primarily focused on maximizing enterprise value and minimizing time commitment on the part of the exiting owners, as these were their two primary goals. The post-transaction assistance was more personal in nature and involved creating specific guidance for each of the owners via FinLife® planning.

Family

Divorce

Divorce impacts about 50% of all marriages. My parents got divorced when I was nine years old, and its impact was extremely deep on me emotionally. In addition to the emotional side, I also felt as if my proverbial roots were torn out of the ground when we relocated from Virginia to Florida. This feeling resonated for years, so much so that when I became an adult I moved back to Virginia and still live there today.

The financial aspects of divorce can be significant and should be evaluated by both parties so that the separation is being approached with all eyes open. To be sure, the nonfinancial issues, such as custody of the children, are every bit as, if not more, important than the financial ramifications. Some things (financial and nonfinancial) to think about: Where will you live? Will the kids have to change schools? Will you have adequate monthly income to pay your bills? Will real estate need to be sold? What about your estate planning? Do you need new insurance? Should you go back to work? What about hiring a child psychologist? Should you pay a professional to talk to?

The next comment I'm going to make is not meant to sound sexist, merely factual based on my experience. What I have found over the years in helping clients with divorce is that the woman in the relationship generally needs an advocate more often than the man. My experience may be a product of the generational group that the couples I have assisted are part of, but regardless, it is what it is. The women that my practice has assisted have relied upon the man as the primary breadwinner in the relationship, and as a result, they do not have the financial power that the man possesses. This has required my firm to take on an advocacy role in making sure that the woman receives what she should receive in a property settlement agreement. This process can be very involved and often necessitates attorneys and forensic work to be done on the financials in order to arrive at a fair arrangement.

If you need any assistance in this area, my business partner, Stan Corey,

CFP, ChFC, has written a best-selling book about the collaborative divorce process titled *The Divorce Dance.*

Real Life FinLife®

We had a client, Pam, who came in as a result of her husband filing divorce papers out of the clear blue sky. As a result, the emotions that rose to the surface were raw, and Pam felt as if her world had been literally turned upside down. To make matters worse, after some initial discovery and research by the Money Navigator, it was determined that the husband had secretly been moving money for several years into an offshore bank account that Pam had no idea about. Literally millions of dollars were uncovered in this account, and we ensured that Pam would be privy to her rightful share of these dollars since they were considered marital assets.

Death of a Spouse

How do you even begin to prepare for this event that ostensibly 50% of the married population in the world will confront? I don't think you can prepare for this eventuality emotionally, but from a FinLife® perspective, you certainly can. You should have "lifeboat drill" conversations with your advisor so each spouse is prepared in advance and knows exactly what to do and who to call if one spouse passes away. This involves being educated on the finances and prepared regarding the to-dos when the inevitable occurs.

Real Life FinLife®

By meeting with their Money Navigator regularly, Tim and Sheila were prepared for any financial eventuality. Sheila had never really participated in the couple's financial affairs prior to their relationship with our firm. That all changed after their Honest Conversations® meeting when Sheila indicated to Tim that even though they had been married over forty years, she never had felt comfortable with the fact that she hadn't known the full financial picture. Over the course of the next couple of years, we actively brought Sheila into the conversations so she understood the structure of their estate, how the investments were allocated and where they were, what types of insurance policies they owned and why, and finally, what their tax situation was and the contact information for their

CPA. This provided Sheila with clarity and confidence going forward so if something happened to Tim, she wouldn't have to scramble to figure things out financially and knew that all she needed to do was to call us and everything would be taken care of. Needless to say, Tim did, in fact, pass away suddenly not too long after Sheila's financial indoctrination. The emotional toll was devastating, as the couple was extremely close; they had been high school sweethearts. We continue to help Sheila with her FinLife® and have made an indelible impression upon the family in a multigenerational fashion, as all three of Tim and Sheila's adult children now work with us as well.

Death of a Parent

The majority of the time, parents die before their children. Sometimes the death of a parent comes as a complete shock, and other times it has been anticipated as a result of old age or illness. When a parent dies, many times an adult child is tasked with the responsibility of serving as the executor of the estate or, if a trust exists, the trustee. This is no small undertaking, and like life, there isn't a training manual provided. As executor, there are times, depending upon the state's probate laws, that you would have to appear in probate court, which is the process of proving the validity of your parent's will. Other times, if you are serving as trustee and you have siblings, this can become contentious, as everyone can have their own needs and concerns. In addition to the asset disposition issues, initially, a more pressing need is the funeral and all that is entailed with that aspect of experiencing the death of a parent. The bottom line is that advance planning by your parents can alleviate a lot of the stress and strain that inevitably occurs as a result of a parent passing away. Emotions are raw during the time immediately following a parent's death, so anything that can be done to minimize the ancillary administrative issues is appreciated by the executor or trustee.

Real Life FinLife®
They showed up at Arlington National Cemetery to bury their father, a decorated army general. The six adult children all came to the funeral, as did the fifteen grandchildren. They were burying the family patriarch, the man who always made everything all right and who made everyone feel

special. This was the legacy that he left behind. Their Money Navigator was there too, as he had been for the general's wife's funeral a few years back. He was part of the family and certainly not considered an outsider. A couple weeks after the 21-gun salute at the culmination of the burial with full honors, the Money Navigator found himself in a conference room with the six children. He had gathered everyone there to discuss the next steps in the estate planning process, which involved the disposition of the family assets. There was an overwhelming feeling of gratitude in the air that morning. Gratitude toward their father and mother for certain. But there was also a sense of gratitude for the Local Navigator and the calm he brought to the storm they all had been experiencing for the last couple of weeks. As he explained the plan to the children, it was almost as if Dad were still in the room speaking to them, and you know what, I think he was.

Loaning a Relative or Friend Money

"She's my cousin and I have the money, so what's the big deal?" Quite a lot, actually. First off, my experience with clients and non-arm's-length transactions such as loans made to their family or friends has not been good. To be sure, yes, there are legitimate borrowers who will pay funds back to a relative or friend, but that has been more of the exception than the rule. More often than not, the debtor ends up appealing to the emotions of the lender to the point of the loan defaulting. The reason this happens is if the money is being borrowed by someone close to the lender, it is being done because the borrower tries to use their relationship as a manipulation tool to get the funds in the first place.

If you do end up lending funds to someone, be sure to have an actual promissory note (a simple one-pager is fine) drafted that indicates the terms of the loan. This way everyone understands that the loan is being treated as a legitimate debt and not simply a favor. This will greatly increase the odds of repayment in a timely fashion.

Real Life FinLife®
Not a lot to say about this except don't go there, unless you are comfortable making a gift (this means you are willing to part with your money that you "loaned" your buddy or sister).

Helping the Kids with Planning

Should the kids (in this case, adult children) work with their parent's financial advisor? This can make a lot of sense for a number of reasons. First, it can put the children on a nice trajectory, from a financial perspective, so they start early in addressing financial issues and concerns, which can give them a head start on living a productive FinLife®. Second, working with their parents' financial advisor provides cohesiveness in the ability of their planning to relate to their parents' planning. One example of this is in regard to asset allocation decisions. If the parents have a large percentage of holdings in stocks that eventually will be inherited by the children, perhaps it makes sense for the children to hold more bonds than they otherwise would normally hold, for diversification purposes. It all depends on the situation, of course, but these are things to consider. Finally, continuity is achieved if the children and parents have the same advisor. The overall planning discussions can involve multiple generations sitting around the table discussing the impact of various strategies and techniques and the ramifications of utilizing said methods.

Real Life FinLife®

When David passed away, his three adult children came to see David's Money Navigator. The Money Navigator and his team had been working with David for two decades, so David's financial house was in perfect order. Roger, Jack, and Elizabeth, David's children, all came to see the Money Navigator upon David's passing. Roger and Jack had already been working with the Money Navigator. However, Elizabeth had her own planner, an insurance agent who worked for a large multinational corporation. The plan that David had developed with the Money Navigator dovetailed into Roger's and Jack's plans nicely. Trusts had been established, as well as 529 plans for college education, and a real estate partnership could continue as planned without any hiccups. Elizabeth, on the other hand, ended up having to establish new accounts and restructure her entire plan because she had decided not to be part of the longer-term planning discussions in which David had invited all of the kids to participate. This caused her a substantial amount of stress and resulted in her allocating significant time and money to get everything in order. Needless to say, having the two boys' plans in the same office made things meld seamlessly for them during an otherwise particularly emotional time.

House and Home

Budgeting

Most people don't enjoy budgeting. I prefer to call it a spending plan because, after all, isn't that what we are more concerned about anyway? That is certainly what our research uncovered in chapter 1. At its core, a spending plan is designed to ensure that you are recording and subsequently prioritizing your expenditures so that you can live within your means, save for your future, and not go unnecessarily into debt. It's easy to build out a spending plan, as many off-the-shelf software packages such as Quicken are available for budgeting. Quicken's user interface is easy to use, and it can sync up with other software applications such as TurboTax and Excel.

Real Life FinLife®
Jessica's son, Andy, recently graduated from college and got his first job. Jessica approached her Local Navigator about sitting down with Andy to establish a budget. In addition to student loans, Andy had racked up $8,000 in credit card debt during his last year in college. Their Local Navigator helped Andy build out a spending plan that not only enabled him to pay down his debts, but also to live a bit as well by making the process fun and rewarding. For example, instead of always going out to lunch, this Local Navigator showed Andy how making his lunch five days a week would impact his plan so he could save enough for Friday evening happy hours with his buddies. Simple solution, yes, but this was not apparent to Andy as he was immersed in the situation. He also had Andy agree to increase his 401k contributions by a certain percentage of whatever raise he received in the future.

Lease or Buy a Car?

It's certainly tempting to lease an automobile these days, as the car dealers have successfully appealed to our greed and desire of owning a nicer vehicle than we otherwise might not be able to afford. That said, it may make sense to lease a car versus buying one outright, depending upon your personal set of circumstances. Do you own your own business, for example? How often do you replace your cars? Do you like to have the latest and greatest technology? These are but a few of the questions you should ask yourself when weighing the pros and cons of leasing a car.

Real Life FinLife®

Have you seen the new Tesla Model 3? In addition to being electric and loaded with super-cool, cutting-edge gadgets, it drives itself using autonomous driving technology. To be sure, the Tesla Model 3 is not inexpensive, and the Money Navigator recommended that his client, John, lease the car because he knew that John preferred to drive only late-model cars and replace them every two to three years. The Money Navigator also knew that John would use the car about 75% for business purposes and as such would receive a nice tax break on the lease payments.

Buy or Rent?

The knee-jerk reaction I commonly see when someone sells their home and relocates after retiring is to buy another home in the new location. You should consider the fact that there is no need to rush into buying another home. It would be more prudent to spend a considerable amount of time in the new area, and even live there for a while, before deciding to make a new real estate purchase. There is nothing wrong with renting a place for a year to get your bearings. You may realize you don't even want to live there, so you'd end up having to sell a house you just purchased. Additionally, you may not want to invest in real estate again. By renting you can be much more agile and mobile in your retirement. You may want to have rentals in a few areas around the country, or the world, for that matter. This gives you a lot of optionality and flexibility. Now, to be clear, I am not saying that you shouldn't buy a home in retirement; I'm simply saying you should consider alternatives. There are certainly advantages to home ownership from a quality of life perspective as well as financial and tax motivations.

Real Life FinLife®

The house just sold, and Chris and Michelle received the proceeds with no taxes owed. The Local Navigator discussed the idea of renting in retirement in lieu of home ownership, and the couple was intrigued. Prior to this discussion, Chris and Michelle felt comfortable making a down payment on a new home, so under this scenario they would take out a mortgage. Payments on the mortgage, including property taxes and insurance, would be affordable. Let's assume rent for a similar-sized home would be about the same as the mortgage payment, so the possibilities were cash-flow neutral. The couple liked the idea of renting and not tying up any of their newfound equity in a new home. Additionally, they had the funds invested in a well-diversified portfolio designed for growth and income in retirement. This portfolio provided additional income for them to travel more and to rent a cabin for one month a year in Vermont, something their Money Navigator knew that Chris and Michelle had always desired.

Paying Off the House

Seems to make sense: pay off all debts, including your mortgage, so you can sleep easier at night. Home ownership has exemplified the American dream since the beginning of this country. Home ownership, however, does not have to mean ownership outright without any encumbrances. From a qualitative perspective, you may feel much better knowing that your home is debt-free and this gives you financial peace. From a quantitative perspective, however, if interest rates are low, as they have been for quite some time now, it makes sense to have a mortgage on your home. If your home is paid off in its entirety, you are sitting on what I like to call dead equity. In that case, the equity in your home is literally trapped within the four walls of your house. On the other hand, if you have a mortgage at a very low interest rate, you are essentially using other people's money (the bank's) for less than 3%, after factoring in the tax-deductibility of the interest. Over the long-term, you should be able to outperform the sub-3% interest rate in a well-diversified portfolio. To be clear, this is the left-brain answer to this issue, and as I've discussed in chapter 5, the right brain often can add quite a bit of context and clarity to the situation.

Real Life FinLife®

Kate recently retired and decided that she wanted to live in the country about an hour or so from the city in which she had lived for her entire working career. This entailed selling her current home and buying a new, more affordable home with more land and establishing herself in a new community. The proceeds she would be receiving from the sale of her existing home would be sufficient to pay off the new home in cash. The client's FinLife® plan worked well regardless of whether or not she paid off the new home or took out a mortgage in retirement. Kate listened to the Money Navigator discuss the pros and cons mentioned above and decided on the quantitative left-brain methodology, whereby she took out a mortgage. The point here is she was provided with choices, and she decided that she didn't need the house paid off in order to sleep at night. The Money Navigator pointed out to Kate that even though she wasn't physically paying off the house, she had the money to pay off the mortgage at any point in the future.

Buying a Second Home

You've always dreamed of having the country house, the mountain getaway, or the lake retreat. Perhaps considering the purchase of a second home is in order. How great would it be to be able to, at a moment's notice, get in the car and drive to your cabin in the mountains? Sounds pretty great, I know. You may be thinking about all of the fun things that you'll be able to do there and all of the amazing memories you will make as a family. One of the distinct benefits of second home ownership is the ability to establish traditions. Traditions resonate with children and provide them with a strong foundational element as they grow up. Traditions provide emotional anchors that kids can hang onto as they mature and become young adults.

Before you sign on the dotted line, you'll want to think about the fact that a lot goes into owning a second home. The obvious one is you have now taken on an additional financial commitment to not only purchase the home but to maintain it as well as visit the property for your memory-making vacations. Also, if you end up renting the property (you are now officially a landlord), that brings in a whole host of other challenges as well as potential opportunities.

Real Life FinLife®

At face value, buying a second home sounds fantastic. That's exactly what Jerry and Anne thought when they purchased their lake house. Visions of family vacations and fun times popped into the couple's head when they contemplated making the down payment on the property. They also thought the home would be a good investment over time, as properties on the lake had continued to increase in price over the past several years. They had the funds set aside to afford it, so why not? The Money Navigator showed Jerry and Anne that the home was affordable, and after purchasing it, their FinLife® plan was funded to a level that provided them with confidence in the plan's ability to still succeed. In other words, under this particular scenario, this was an affordable discretionary investment that made sense for them from a quantitative and qualitative perspective. The Local Navigator provided the client with clarity about the situation, which in turn provided them with confidence to move forward.

Money Management and Insurance

Tax-Efficient Investing

The premise here is quite simple. When investing for tax efficiency, it is imperative that concern for taxes is woven through every single investment strategy in the portfolio. Failing to acknowledge the tax impact of investing is something many planners routinely do, albeit many times unknowingly. The savings from properly investing in a tax-efficient manner is significant, and its impact on returns long term cannot be overstated.

Real Life FinLife®

The Money Navigator explained to his client, Tim, that tax loss harvesting is one of the best ways to achieve the goal of tax efficiency within the construct of his investment strategy. This concept, although simple, is unfortunately not used with the frequency that it should be. The Money Navigator provided Tim with estimates of realized and unrealized gains and losses prior to year's end. If Tim's net realized gains appeared to be higher than anticipated, an analysis of unrealized losses could be made and certain securities could be sold in an attempt to match realized losses with realized gains—not a complicated idea, but one often neglected by many advisors. The Local Navigator is cognizant of the impact of tax loss harvesting on Tim's overall returns. He also knows that establishing a free-flow of information between him and Tim's CPA is critical, so open communication occurs while relieving Tim of having to administratively deal with sourcing tax documents such as K-1s and 1099s.

Stock Options or Restricted Stock Units (RSUs)

Do you potentially have a concentrated position in a stock as a result of owning stock options or restricted stock units (RSUs)? This is the case for many employees who own stock options and RSUs. If so, it may be a good idea to consider setting up a systematic exercise schedule in order to move out of the stock and into a more diversified portfolio. If the position is a considerable percentage of your overall net worth, it means that your portfolio is at greater risk of being impacted if something negative happens to the company, the industry in which the company operates, or the stock market in general. These risks can be mitigated by moving out of the money stock as the options vest or as the RSUs mature.

Real Life FinLife®
Remove the emotion from the process. Easier said than done. Donald had a few million dollars in stock options. The Money Navigator convinced Donald to exercise the vested options and redeploy the funds into a well-diversified portfolio. Donald's friend waited another year to exercise and pocketed more than Donald did a year earlier with the same amount of options. Another year went by and the stock had dropped about 80% in value and Donald's friend was devastated. Why would he be devastated since he got out of the stock a year earlier? Well, he hadn't sold the stock that he obtained by exercising the options, but instead had held onto the shares, counting on them to increase greatly in value. His DIY planning had lost him a considerable amount of money.

Insurance

I covered the foundational importance of having proper insurance coverage in chapter 7. Nobody likes to talk about insurance, and can you blame them? Who wants to admit that they are vulnerable? That said, confronting insurance and accepting that you need it requires you to let your guard down and open up in ways that make you uncomfortable. But the sooner you admit that you should at least evaluate insurance for your personal set of circumstances, the better. Otherwise you risk having your FinLife® plan crumbling from unexpected death or disability.

Real Life FinLife®

The Money Navigator has a client who is extremely adventurous. One day, Frank was enjoying time snow skiing with family and friends. During the course of the day, he had done all sorts of fun things with his family, from skiing and hiking to snowmobiling. As the day went on, there came a point where the family ended up at another friend's house that they had not visited before. Just for fun, Frank decided to jump off the roof of the house into the snow. The snow was piled up several feet high, so it seemed safe. Unfortunately, what Frank didn't know was that there was a rock outcropping just below the snow. Needless to say, this otherwise benign event left an indelible mark on the client's life, as he became paralyzed from the waist down as a result of his decision to jump. The tie-in regarding insurance here should be obvious, but in case it is not, disability insurance enabled Frank to continue to support his family even though a tragic accident (and poor judgment) disabled him and prohibited him from working.

LTC Insurance for Parents

We are all living longer, a lot longer. Our parents are likely to outlive their parents by a significant number of years. With that longevity comes the increased likelihood that our parents will require some type of long-term care. This could be home health care, assisted living, Alzheimer's care, or nursing home care. These costs are not inexpensive and unfortunately, as we talked about in chapter 7, they are not covered by Medicare or private health insurance with any degree of significance. This leaves it up to us to either self-insure against these expenses or to purchase long-term care insurance. What plans do your parents have to cover long-term care expenditures? If they can self-insure, consider them fortunate. If they have purchased long-term care insurance, consider them pragmatic. If they cannot do either, then you may be called upon at some point to intervene. This happens every day across our nation, and it creates a substantial amount of stress and strain emotionally and financially.

Real Life FinLife®
Long-term care insurance was purchased by Nancy to minimize the impact of a long-term care illness on her estate. After several years of paying the insurance premiums, Nancy started to find it difficult financially to continue to make the premium payments. Her Money Navigator discussed this in detail with her, and they collectively determined that there were essentially three viable choices going forward. The first was to let the policy lapse by no longer paying the premiums. This was the least desirable for Nancy. The second was to purchase an immediate income annuity that would generate enough annual income to pay the policy premium. Nancy had enough in assets to make this option realistic. The third was to have her adult children pay for the policy. The thought here was this would help the children preserve their eventual inheritance. After discussing everything with Nancy's children, it was agreed upon to have the children pay the premiums so the coverage would be maintained and their mother's assets preserved.

Retirement

Retirement Now or Later?

You have decided that you are going to work eight more years at your current job until you turn sixty-five, and then you will retire.

Have you thought about what your day would be like if you were retired? If so, what's it like? Paint a vivid picture for yourself. What types of activities are you involved with, and with whom? Where are you living? What is your house like? Your neighborhood? What about your friends? Is your family nearby? Are you traveling at all, and if so, where? What causes are you supporting or volunteering for?

Real Life FinLife®
Donna arrived at her Money Navigator's office after a sleepless night.

She had been referred to the Money Navigator by her sister, Kristi, who had been a long-time client. Kristi had recently retired with the help of the Money Navigator, and since she had always been so close to Donna, she wanted her to receive the same type of advice that she had received. Donna knew that Kristi was better off financially, so she got no sleep the night before because she felt ashamed and embarrassed about her financial situation compared to her sister's, especially since Donna was a few years older. She gathered all of her financial data (something the Money Navigator told her she would not need to do, by the way—as the Money Navigator desires to understand his client fully before delving into the numbers) and brought it to the meeting.

Donna discussed many things with the Money Navigator, but the overriding issue was the fact that she was cash flow negative on a monthly basis due to the fact that she had been forced to change careers due to layoffs and restructurings. Her primary objective was singular in focus— increase her monthly income and lower her expenses. This makes perfect sense because the problem is in the here and now! Instead of jumping on this issue and attacking it head-on, the Money Navigator instead asked a series of questions. By doing so he was able to determine that Donna wanted to retire now. Sounds ridiculous given what I've described about her financial situation so far, I know. That said, Donna owned her own home, and it was worth about $700,000 with about a $100,000 mortgage against it. She also had a fairly sizeable investment account (although it was even larger a few months prior to the meeting but had subsequently declined considerably due to the allocation being far too aggressive for Donna's risk tolerance).

What happened next was nothing short of phenomenal. Donna indicated to the Local Navigator that she wanted to eventually be able to retire near Kristi's new home that she had recently purchased as part of her overall financial plan. She was concerned that it would take about five years of continuing to work before she would be able to transition into retirement. She needed to pay down credit card debts that had been accumulating as a result of her monthly cash flow deficit.

The Money Navigator recommended that Donna sell her house now, buy a house near Kristi for about $300,000, as the new home was in a much more affordable area in the countryside. The difference in equity that she would receive would be about $300,000 (perhaps even more if Donna decided to have a mortgage for tax-efficiency reasons), which would be invested in such a manner as it would drive additional retirement income for Donna. So her portfolio of $900,000 or so would produce enough income coupled with Social Security for Donna to retire today.

After scheduling her next meeting with the Money Navigator to review her plan implementation, she jumped up in the air and yelled out "yes!" She had seen the world through a new lens, brought into focus by the Money Navigator.

Guaranteed Income in Retirement

Ensuring that you'll have enough retirement income is paramount. Some of the income sources you may have are guaranteed or remain fixed over time. This takes the guesswork out of how much money you'll receive each month. Guaranteed income doesn't vary based upon how the stock market is doing or whether or not interest rates are moving up or down. Things like pensions (which are becoming rarer by the day), Social Security, and fixed annuities are the most common sources.

Pensions receive protection from the Pension Benefit Guaranty Corporation (PBGC). The PBGC is a government organization established for the purpose of ensuring that Americans are not cheated out of their hard-earned pension benefits. Pension plans pay premiums into the PBGC so their pensions are insured.

Social Security payments are guaranteed by the federal government, and the system is certainly facing serious fiscal and demographic challenges; however, it is likely that it will still prove to be a dependable income source in retirement for some time to come. The current estimate by the Social Security Administration is that program costs will rise in the next eighteen years so taxes will be enough to pay for only 75% of scheduled benefits.[1]

Fixed annuities provide guaranteed income payments, and they are backed by the financial claims-paying ability of the issuing insurance company.

---

1   S. Goss, "Social Security Administration," retrieved January 04, 2017, https://www.ssa.gov/policy/docs/ssb/v70n3/v70n3p111.html.

Real Life FinLife®

Getting organized is critical in determining your foundational retirement income. The Money Navigator will help you determine how to maximize all of your guaranteed income sources. Peter and Bobbi both had defined benefit pension plans. However, Bobbi's was much smaller than Peter's and represented a minority share of the overall income for the couple. Additionally, Bobbi was ten years younger than Peter. Conventional wisdom says they both should do joint/survivor annuities on their pensions. After all, if one of them died, shouldn't the survivor continue to receive pension benefits from the deceased spouse's pension? For example, if Bobbi's pension was 20% of the overall income in retirement, it makes more sense for her to take a Life Only annuity payment with no survivor (this also assumes that Peter elects a Life with 100% Survivor option on his pension(s)). Subsequently, if Bobbi dies first, Peter will still have 80% of the overall income, which generally should be sufficient in retirement. Additionally, it is likely that Peter dies first (based on life expectancies), so Bobbi will maintain 100% of the overall retirement income for a much longer period of time.

Relocation for Retirement

You are retiring, so you are considering relocating to a different area (state, city, country, etc.). There are many reasons to consider such a move. A warmer climate, the leisure activities available, perceived lifestyle, accessibility of healthcare, affordability of housing, other friends that have moved there, lower cost of living, no state income tax, and lower real estate taxes are several of the reasons you are considering relocating for retirement.

Real Life FinLife®

Instead of relocating to Florida for retirement, their Money Navigator recommended that Jeffrey and Kim sell their existing home and simply downsize to a nice condominium nearby. After many discussions about the topic, the Money Navigator realized that the couple had fallen into a trap of thinking that they had to retire to the warmth of the south. The Money Navigator's strategy removed the home maintenance concerns the couple had articulated as having become far too burdensome, expensive, unpredictable, and time consuming. By moving locally, this also negated the problem of having to establish an entirely new network of friends after they had lived in the same area for thirty years. Additionally, not relocating enabled Jeff and Kim to maintain their current doctors, which was a big concern of theirs as they aged. Finally, staying in town for retirement provided them a way to stay in close touch with their adult children and grandchildren who lived nearby. The home they dreamed of that they would own in Florida now disappeared, but maintaining a new residence in their community and renting a place in Florida for two months out of the year seemed like a much better and more flexible way to go.

Estate Planning Documents

Having current estate planning documents in place is critical. In addition to a will, powers of attorney and medical directives (living will) ensure that your wishes and desires are carried out the way you want them to be. Additionally, having a revocable trust can help your estate avoid the expenses and delay associated with the probate process. Probate is essentially the process of proving the validity of your will in court. Instead, if your assets are owned by a revocable trust, the probate process is avoided in its entirety, saving your heirs countless headaches as well as legal costs and probate fees. Sometimes it is appropriate to have more advanced estate planning documents in place such as an irrevocable trust. Among other benefits, irrevocable trusts are often used to minimize the impact of estate taxes levied against your assets after you pass away. The savings from utilizing proper estate planning documents can range from the thousands to literally millions of dollars.

Real Life FinLife®
Years ago, the Money Navigator's client, Keith, expressed an interest in minimizing his estate taxes. As a result of many planning discussions, the Money Navigator ended up setting up an irrevocable life insurance trust that was not taxed upon his death because the policy was owned outside of his personal estate. After he passed away, the death benefit from the life insurance policy went into the irrevocable trust, and his daughter utilized part of the proceeds to pay the estate tax bill. This enabled her to not have to sell the family farm, which her father wanted her to keep in the

family for future generations. The life insurance also provided money for the daughter to send both of her children to medical school, whereby one became a dentist and the other a physician. The daughter and the dentist remain the Money Navigator's clients to this day.

Planning for Incapacity

Alzheimer's disease, dementia, and other forms of cognitive impairment are quite common and rob you of your ability to effectively make or convey your decisions as you age. As of today, there is no cure for Alzheimer's, but you can take steps in advance in order to protect your estate, income, and overall legacy for your heirs. Most problems with incapacity occur because nothing was stated in writing in advance. This situation becomes extremely difficult and places a burden upon family members to make decisions that ultimately may or may not align with your wishes and desires.

Real Life FinLife®
Sue has been living by herself for the past twenty-five years since she and her husband divorced. About three years ago, during a routine doctor's visit, it was determined that she had early-stage Alzheimer's. Since that time the disease has gotten progressively worse even though Sue has been involved in a clinical trial for a new anti-Alzheimer's medication. Based on the progression of the illness, it is likely that she is receiving a placebo or that the drug simply isn't effective. Once the diagnosis occurred, Sue's adult children took her to see an estate planning attorney on the advice of the Local Navigator. According to her physician, Sue was still able to think for herself and make decisions, so she was legally capable of signing new documents. The critical components were an updated will, powers of attorney (financial and medical), as well as an advanced medical directive (including a living will). Although the will was important, the powers of attorney and advanced medical directive were the most essential documents with respect to her potential incapacitation. Specifically, the powers of attorney would enable her daughters to act on her behalf with respect to her investments, paying her bills, and making healthcare decisions. The living will allowed Sue to make decisions in advance about how she felt about life support systems and resuscitative devices.

More Tools for Your Toolbox

Investments & Savings Vehicles

Mutual Funds

An investment fund that is professionally managed that pools money from many investors and issues shares in exchange for ownership. A mutual fund adjusts its net asset value (NAV) daily after the market closes, meaning it's valued only once per day. Mutual funds are regulated by the Securities and Exchange Commission (SEC) and specifically by the Investment Company Act of 1940. A mutual fund is overseen by a board of directors that ensures that the fund is managed in the best interest of its shareholders. Mutual funds have internal expense structures for the management and marketing of the fund. I'm not a big fan of mutual funds because, quite honestly, when you buy one, you generally are purchasing a manager's five or ten best picks and a bunch of sawdust. What I mean is mutual funds must be diversified and track a benchmark index, which results in a lot of filler being added in order to comply with their prospectus mandates.

Exchange Traded Funds

An investment fund that is traded on public stock exchanges similar to a stock. The majority of ETFs track an index and are popular for being low cost and tax efficient. Unlike a mutual fund, an ETF adjusts its NAV over the course of the trading day so they are recognized as being more nimble than mutual funds. ETFs, due to their majoritively passive investment structure, are less expensive than mutual funds from an internal expense standpoint. I like ETFs, because they are generally low cost and provide broad-based market and sector exposure.

Stocks (equities)

Represents the equity of the owners of a company. Stocks are traded on various exchanges, and they signify a fractional share of the ownership of a business. Investing in stocks is not a guessing game nor a gambling exercise, as many individuals commonly and incorrectly assume. In fact, the value of a share of stock is simply the amount of all future anticipated cash flows from the company discounted back to a present value, which is then divided by the number of shares outstanding. I'm a fan of equities and portfolios that invest in stocks. A good equity manager can add value, or alpha (excess return over a designated benchmark), to your overall portfolio allocation.

Bonds (debt)

Bonds are simple, right? Maybe, but in general, a bond is a vehicle that represents a debt that the issuer owes to the holder. Interest is paid by the issuer until the maturity of the bond, at which time the principal is repaid to the holder. The easiest way to look at this is to think of bond issuers as borrowers and bond investors as lenders. I do not like bond funds because they tend to decline in value precipitously during upward moves in interest rates. I prefer using individual bond ladders to protect portfolios against devaluation and interest rate risk.

Options

A contract that provides the holder the unobligated right to buy or sell an underlying asset at a specified price on or before a specified date. When you purchase or sell an options contract you are expecting the current value of the underlying asset to increase or decrease, which in turn generates a profit for you if you were correct in the movement of the asset's price. I utilize options for clients primarily to hedge concentrated positions that clients are not comfortable fully unwinding.

Cash/Bank Accounts

Money that is held in a checking or savings account guaranteed by the FDIC. You should have anywhere from three to twelve months of cash reserves on hand to cover emergencies, such as noninsured car or home repairs.

Money Market Funds

Are similar to a savings account where the account earns interest and, unlike bank money market *accounts*, money market *funds* are not guaranteed by the FDIC. Money market funds are considered safe, are regulated by the SEC, and generally provide a higher yield than bank deposits. These accounts can be considered part of your emergency reserves, as they are liquid and readily accessible.

Certificates of Deposit

A time deposit that is generally issued by banks and credit unions. CDs are required to be held for a specified period of time or a penalty applies if withdrawn early. Interest rates tend to be higher than other bank instruments that can be withdrawn on demand. CDs are considered to be a conservative investment but should not be considered part of your emergency reserves.

Insurance Contracts

Fixed Annuity

An insurance contract designed to protect you from outliving your money. Fixed annuities grow tax-deferred, avoid probate, and can be withdrawn penalty free after a surrender period, similar to CDs. Additionally, fixed annuities can be annuitized or turned into a series of guaranteed payments over a specified period of time or the remainder of your life. Rates of return are generally higher than CDs, primarily due to the longer surrender schedules offered. There are no internal expense charges in fixed annuities.

Fixed Index Annuity

A type of fixed annuity. In addition to a fixed interest rate option, the contract owner's return can also be pegged to a market index, such as the S&P 500 Index. Caps and participation rates determine how much interest can be credited to your account either monthly or annually, and

your principal is protected against market losses. Similar to fixed annuities, FIAs can be annuitized. Generally speaking, FIAs have no internal
expense charges unless an income rider is elected. FIAs are great tools that
can be used as volatility dampeners in your portfolio.

Variable Annuity

A type of annuity that enables the contract holder to invest in mutual
fund–like sub-accounts. The principal is not guaranteed, unlike fixed
and fixed index annuities. Variable annuities can be annuitized (turned
into a guaranteed series of payments for life or over a specified period
of time). However, the income amount can fluctuate depending upon
the performance of the underlying sub-accounts. Variable annuities have
internal expense charges for the management of the sub-accounts as well
as mortality and other expenses.

Permanent Life Insurance

A life insurance contract that covers the remaining life of the insured. A
cash value is associated with the policy, and the owner can access this cash
during his lifetime via withdrawals, loans, or by surrendering the contract.
There are four primary flavors—whole life, universal life, indexed universal life, and variable life.

Term Life Insurance

A life insurance contract that covers the insured for a specified period of
time and then expires. This form of insurance is more cost effective than
permanent insurance.

Long-Term Care Insurance

An insurance policy that provides coverage to the insured for the costs of
a long-term care illness. LTC costs are generally not covered by Medicare
or private health insurance, which has led to the popularity of LTC
insurance.

Disability Insurance

A form of insurance that covers an individual for loss of income due to a
disabling event. There are two types, short-term disability and long-term
disability.

Important Disclosure

The information discussed or opinions provided are those of the author and do not necessarily reflect the opinions of United Capital Financial Advisors, LLC (United Capital), its affiliates, subsidiaries, or the management thereof. Information provided by third parties has not been independently verified by United Capital and is treated as accurate. United Capital provides financial life management and makes recommendations based on the specific needs and circumstances of each client. For clients with managed accounts, United Capital has discretionary authority over investment decisions. Investing involves risk, and clients should carefully consider their own investment objectives and never rely on any single chart, graph, or book to make decisions. Certain statements contained within are forward-looking statements including, but not limited to, predictions or indications of future events, trends, plans, or objectives. Undue reliance should not be placed on such statements because, by their nature, they are subject to known and unknown risks and uncertainties. Opinions expressed are current as of the date of this publication and are subject to change. The information contained in this book is intended for information purposes only, is not a recommendation to buy or sell any securities, and should not be considered investment advice. Please contact your financial advisor with questions about your specific needs and circumstances. One Best Financial Life®, FinLife®, Honest Converations®, and Money Mind® are registered trademarks of United Capital.

Index

BARBARA'S BOOKSTORE
CHICAGO O'HARE AIRPORT
2309 MOUNT PROSPECT RD.
DES PLAINES, IL 60018
STORE: 00840 REG: 001 CASHIER: Sadiq
CUSTOMER RECEIPT COPY

MONEY NAVIGATOR
9781626344419 1 @ 23.95   23.95
SUBTOTAL   23.95
SALES TAX (10.25000%)   2.46
TOTAL   **26.41**

AMOUNT TENDERED

Visa   **26.41**
  SALE
  ACCT: ************7530
  EXP: ******
  APPROVAL: H95256
  ENTRY METHOD: SWIPED

TOTAL PAYMENT   26.41
Transaction: 35917   10/20/2017 7:25 PM
    Comments\Inquiries? (800) 326-7711
      or Comments@Hudsongroup.com
    Thank you for shopping with us.

03591700840001102 02017

About the Author

Paul Bennett is a CERTIFIED FINANCIAL PLANNER™ professional (CFP®), Chartered Financial Consultant (ChFC®), and Managing Director of the United Capital regional office in Great Falls, Virginia. He holds a PhD in economics, with distinction, from SMC University, an MS in finance, with honors, from Indiana University, and a BA from the University of Florida. He will complete a postdoctoral MS in applied analytics from Columbia University in 2017.

Paul is a three-time author, as he has written two previously published books: *Financial Economics of Index Annuities: An Analysis of Investor Returns* (ISBN: 1612334083) and *Easy Essays on Economics* (ISBN: 1612332692). He is quoted often in the press and has contributed to various publications such as *U.S. News and World Report*, CNBC.com, *Dow Jones News*, *Financial Advisor Magazine*, *Financial Planning Magazine*, *Investment News*, *Washingtonian* magazine, and *The Washington Post*. He also has served as a subject matter expert for the Certified Financial Planner Board of Standards, contributing to the development of examination questions for the CFP® Certification Examination and analyzing the tasks of CFP® designees for the CFP® Job Analysis Work Group.

Paul resides in Great Falls, Virginia, with his wife and twins. In his free time he enjoys traveling with his family, reading nonfiction, and playing an occasional round of golf.